Bloom's

GUIDES

Kurt Vonnegut's
Slaughterhouse-Five

CURRENTLY AVAILABLE

The Adventures of Huckleberry Finn
All the Pretty Horses
Animal Farm
Beloved
Brave New World
The Catcher in the Rye
The Chosen
The Crucible
Cry, the Beloved Country
Death of a Salesman
Fahrenheit 451
The Glass Menagerie
The Grapes of Wrath
Great Expectations
The Great Gatsby
Hamlet
The Handmaid's Tale
The House on Mango Street
I Know Why the Caged Bird Sings
The Iliad
Lord of the Flies
Macbeth
Maggie: A Girl of the Streets
The Member of the Wedding
The Metamorphosis
Of Mice and Men
1984
The Odyssey
One Hundred Years of Solitude
Pride and Prejudice
Ragtime
Romeo and Juliet
Slaughterhouse-Five
The Scarlet Letter
Snow Falling on Cedars
A Streetcar Named Desire
A Tale of Two Cities
The Things They Carried
To Kill a Mockingbird

Bloom's
GUIDES

Kurt Vonnegut's
Slaughterhouse-Five

Edited & with an Introduction
by Harold Bloom

CHELSEA HOUSE
PUBLISHERS
An imprint of Infobase Publishing

Bloom's Guides: Slaughterhouse-Five

Copyright © 2007 by Infobase Publishing
Introduction © 2007 by Harold Bloom

Chelsea House
An imprint of Infobase Publishing
132 West 31st Street
New York NY 10001

Library of Congress Cataloging-in-Publication Data
Kurt Vonnegut's Slaughterhouse-five / Harold Bloom, editor.
        p. cm — (Bloom's guides)
        Includes bibliographical references and index.
        ISBN 0-7910-9295-X
        1. Vonnegut, Kurt. Slaughterhouse five. I. Bloom, Harold.
    II. Title: Slaughterhouse-five.
    PS3572.O5S6356 2007
    813'.54—dc22   2006025339

Chelsea House books are available at special discounts when purchased in bulk quantities for businesses, associations, institutions, or sales promotions. Please call our Special Sales Department in New York at (212) 967-8800 or (800) 322-8755.

You can find Chelsea House on the World Wide Web at
http://www.chelseahouse.com

Contributing Editor: Neil Heims
Cover design by Takeshi Takahashi

Printed in the United States of America
Bang EJB 10 9 8 7 6 5 4 3 2 1

This book is printed on acid-free paper.

All links and web addresses were checked and verified to be correct at the time of publication. Because of the dynamic nature of the web, some addresses and links may have changed since publication and may no longer be valid.

Contents

 Introduction

HAROLD BLOOM

On December 19, 1944, Kurt Vonnegut was captured by the Germans during the Battle of the Bulge; he was 22 years old. Sent to Dresden, he survived the firebombing of the city on February 13–14, 1945, in which 135,000 Germans were killed. That is the biographical context (in part) for the novel, *Slaughterhouse-Five, or The Children's Crusade* (1969).

Since Vonnegut had begun publishing novels in 1952, it is clear that nearly a quarter-century had to go by before the trauma of 1945 could be transmuted into the exorcism of *Slaughterhouse-Five*. I have just reread the novel after thirty years, remembering my shocked admiration for it when it first appeared, and not looking forward to encountering it again. As it should, *Slaughterhouse-Five* remains a very disturbed and disturbing book, and still moves me to troubled admiration. I prefer *Cat's Cradle*, but *Slaughterhouse-Five* may prove to be an equally permanent achievement.

The shadow of Céline's *Journey to the End of the Night* never quite leaves Vonnegut's starker works, including *Slaughterhouse-Five*. I myself read the anti-Semitic Céline with loathing; one sees what is strong in the writing, but a Jewish literary critic is hardly Céline's ideal audience. So it goes.

It is difficult to comment upon *Slaughterhouse-Five* without being contaminated by its styles and procedures, which is necessarily a tribute to the book. In "structure" (an absurd term to apply to almost any novel by Vonnegut), *Slaughterhouse-Five* is a whirling medley, and yet it all coheres. Billy Pilgrim, as a character, does not cohere, but that is appropriate, since his schizophrenia (to call it that) is central to the book.

The planet Tralfamadore, where Billy enjoys pneumatic bliss with Montana Wildhack, is certainly preferable to a world of Nazi death camps and Dresden firebombings. The small miracle of *Slaughterhouse-Five* is that it could be composed at all. Vonnegut always writes from the survivor's stance, where all laughter has to be a step away from madness or fury. So indeed it goes.

Somewhere in the book, the Tralfamadorians tell Billy Pilgrim that their flying-saucer crews had verified the presence of seven sexes on Earth, all of them necessary if babies are to go on being born. I think that is one of the useful moral observations I will keep in mind whenever I recall *Slaughterhouse-Five*.

Biographical Sketch

Kurt Vonnegut, Jr. was born in Indianapolis, Indiana, on November 11, 1922. His mother, Edith, was the daughter of a wealthy brewer; his father was a prominent architect. With the Depression of 1929, the family suffered a serious financial setback. Without work, his father was forced to sell their luxurious home, and they lived in considerably reduced circumstances. Both his father and mother became quite despondent, his mother so much so that on May 14, 1944, she committed suicide by taking an overdose of sleeping pills. After her death, until his own on October 1, 1957, Kurt Vonnegut, Sr. withdrew rather completely into himself.

Young Kurt Vonnegut was withdrawn from private school and attended public schools. He went to Shortridge High in Indianapolis and began writing there for the *Daily Echo*, of which he became the editor. In 1940, after graduation, he enrolled at Cornell University in upstate New York. At his father's urging, he was a biology and chemistry major, like his elder brother, Bernard, who became a pioneer rainmaker by discovering a way to "seed" clouds. Vonnegut, however, did not have an academic aptitude for the sciences. He did, however, become the managing editor of the *Cornell Daily Sun* and a regular columnist for the paper. In 1943, in the midst of the Second World War, before being asked to leave Cornell because of poor academic performance, Vonnegut enlisted in the army. On December 22, 1944, he was taken prisoner by the Germans at the Battle of the Bulge, an attempt by more than half a million German troops to break through the Allied lines in the Ardennes, a wooded plateau extending through France, Belgium, and Luxemburg. Hitler's armies suffered an overwhelming defeat, however, in January 1945. Over 100,000 men were killed or wounded, and the Allies suffered grave casualties, too, with around 81,000 killed or wounded.

Vonnegut was taken to Dresden where he was among prisoners incarcerated in the cellar of a slaughterhouse and made to work in a factory that manufactured vitamin syrup for pregnant women. An "open city," Dresden, known as the Florence of the east and famous for its beautiful architecture and for the china produced there, had no military installations, manufactured no military equipment, and had no military defenses. On February 13, 1945, Vonnegut was there, in the shelter of the slaughterhouse meat locker, when British and American airplanes strafed the city and dropped tons of phosphorous bombs on it, killing more than 135,000 of its inhabitants and completely destroying Dresden by fire.

Vonnegut was repatriated on May 22, 1945, by Russian troops. He returned to the United States and, on September first, married Jane Marie Cox, whom he had known since their days in kindergarten together. They lived in Chicago. Vonnegut was a graduate student at the University of Chicago studying anthropology and worked as a police reporter for the *Chicago City News*. As at Cornell, he did not thrive academically at Chicago, and when his Master's thesis, "On the Fluctuations between Good and Evil in Simple Tales" was unanimously rejected, he and Jane moved to Schenectady, New York, in 1947, where Vonnegut got a job as a publicist for General Electric. That same year, their son, Mark was born and, in 1949, their daughter Edith was born.

Vonnegut continued to write while he worked for GE and, on February 11, 1950, *Collier's Magazine*, a popular mass-circulation magazine of the time, published his short story, "Report on the Barnhouse Effect." It was an auspicious beginning. Vonnegut sold additional stories to *Colliers, The Saturday Evening Post, Ladies' Home Journal*, and other magazines, and within a year he was able to quit his job with General Electric and move his family to West Barnstable in Cape Cod, Massachusetts. In 1952, *Player Piano*, his first novel was published. In 1954, his daughter, Nanette, was born and between 1954 and 1956, Vonnegut taught English at the Hopefield School in Massachusetts, a school for emotionally troubled students, wrote copy for an advertising agency, and opened a Saab automobile dealership, the first in the United States, at a time when foreign cars truly were foreign. In 1957, his father died, and in 1958, his sister, Alice, died of cancer at the age of forty-one, less than forty-eight hours after her husband had been killed in a train accident. After their deaths, Vonnegut adopted three of his sister's four orphaned children. In 1959, his second novel, *The Sirens of Titan* was published. In 1961, he produced a collection of short stories titled *Canary in a Cat House*, and over the next two years his novels *Mother Night* and *Cat's Cradle* appeared. Between 1965 and 1967 he was Writer-in-Residence at the University of Iowa's Writer's Workshop, and he published his fifth novel, *God Bless You, Mr. Rosewater, or Pearls Before Swine*. In 1967, Vonnegut traveled to Dresden on a Guggenheim Fellowship, where he did research for *Slaughterhouse-Five*, his best known novel, which was published in 1969, following his second collection of short stories, *Welcome to the Monkey House*, published in 1968.

The success of *Slaughterhouse-Five* left Vonnegut depressed, particularly by the painful intensity of his recollection of the firebombing of Dresden, and he considered perhaps that he had written all the novels he had in him. He concentrated on teaching creative writing at Harvard, and finished a play, *Happy Birthday, Wanda June*. It played in its initial run off-Broadway for six months to mixed notices and has often been staged since. In 1971, the University of Chicago awarded him a Master's degree for *Cat's Cradle* for its contribution to cultural anthropology. That year, too, his son Mark, suffered what was called a schizophrenic breakdown after several bad LSD trips and was being treated in a hospital in California. Mark wrote *The Eden Express: A Memoir of Insanity*, about his collapse and recovery. It was published in 1975. He became a physician.

In 1972, Kurt Vonnegut, separated from his wife, moved to New York City by himself, and was elected vice-president of P.E.N. American center. P.E.N. is an organization of Playwrights, Poets, Essayists, Editors, and Novelists devoted to advancing the cause of free speech and supporting writers throughout the world who are subject to any sort of censorship or persecution because of their writing. Social engagement was not new to him. In his novels he wrote against conformity, materialism, and the dehumanization of corporate culture. Vonnegut was and continues into his eighties, to be publicly outspoken as a pacifist and a socialist. He opposed the Vietnam War and both the first and the second Iraq wars. In 1970, he traveled to Biafra during the civil war in Nigeria. He also testified in 1986 at the Attorney General's Commission on Pornography Hearing in support of the National Coalition Against Censorship.

In 1973, Vonnegut did publish another novel, *Breakfast of Champions*, which was a popular and commercial success, although critics dismissed it as a lesser work. That year, too, he was appointed Distinguished Professor of English Prose by the City University of New York. In 1974, a collection of his essays and speeches, *Wampeters, Foma & Granfalloons* was published and Vonnegut was awarded an honorary doctorate of literature by Hobart and William Smith College. In 1975, he was elected Vice President of the National Institute of Arts and Letters. In 1979, Vonnegut divorced his wife and married Jill Kremetz, a writer and photographer. They filed for divorce in 1991, but then withdrew the petition. Despite periods of anguish, depression, and writing slumps—he attempted suicide by pills and alcohol in 1984—Vonnegut has continued to write novels, stories, essays, autobiographical pieces, and a children's book. In addition he began drawing and exhibiting his drawings in the eighties. He published two novels in the nineties, *Hocus Pocus* (1990) and *Timequake* (1997). And all his novels have remained in print. In addition, his work has been adapted for the movies, television and the stage. He was named New York State Author by The New York State Writers Institute in 2001.

The Story Behind the Story

That the story behind the story is included in the novel significantly defines the kind of non-linear, loose-boundaried, self-reflexive but socially engaged writer Kurt Vonnegut is and the kind of novel *Slaughterhouse-Five* is. Its presence there alerts the reader to something about the story that readers might otherwise overlook, that the way Vonnegut tells the story is a significant part of the story itself.

The story of *Slaughterhouse-Five* is the story of a man's response—or of his difficulty in making a response—to the firebombing of Dresden in 1945, near the end of the Second World War. While it is Vonnegut's firm conviction that all war is malicious, mad, and unspeakably horrifying, the incineration of Dresden, a jewel among the cities of Europe and with no military significance, and the slaughter of more than 135,000 of its population achieved for him an emblematic and utterly inexpressible status, which he endeavors in the novel both to express and to demonstrate its inexpressibility.

Vonnegut had been in Dresden, as a prisoner of war, when Allied airplanes destroyed it. He did not perish because he was sheltered in a meat locker in the sub-basement of a slaughterhouse where he was incarcerated. After the bombing was completed and those who escaped death could emerge, Vonnegut was assigned by his German captors to a crew whose job was to round up the dead and burn the bodies.

After the war he was haunted by his experience of Dresden, perplexed by the problem of how to speak of it and troubled by what to say of it. The issue confronting him was how to live in a world where such massive and senseless manmade death happens. By his own admission, he wrote and wrote about his experience but nothing he wrote was adequate. When he contacted the United States Air Force to learn everything he could about the air strike—the planning that went into it, the rationale for it, the effect, the number killed and wounded—the only response he got to his inquiry was that all information about the bombing of Dresden was classified.

Nevertheless, perhaps, even, consequently, Vonnegut continued to pursue the project of writing about Dresden, focusing on his own memories. He also, with the aid of a Guggenheim grant, returned to Dresden in 1967, to see the city first hand and to do research there. When he finally could write about Dresden, Vonnegut incorporated the history of his attempts to write about it and the impossibility of writing about it into *Slaughterhouse-Five*. Thus, although *Slaughterhouse-Five* rests on the solid foundation of his research and his first-hand experience, its power as a novel about Dresden comes rather from the manner in which it was written and by the writer's combination of outrage and absurdity, and by his confession inside the book that the book is "lousy," that is, inadequate.

The novel itself is characterized by the apparently contradictory traits that impelled Vonnegut to write it and the forces that stymied him. *Slaughterhouse-Five* shows an intensely focused concentration on the subject, which is achieved through the continuous return to the war narrative inside the novel. However, it is also characterized by a continuous sense of being distracted from his subject, of avoiding it through the interruption of the Dresden narrative by slipping into other narratives. This vacillation represents not only the structure of the novel but the structure of the psyche of the novel's main character, Billy Pilgrim and of Vonnegut himself who introduces himself in his own person into the novel as the narrator. The complexity of this narrative conflict actually is a part of the Dresden story. It shows the contradictions inherent in any response to the attack. Vonnegut's narrative insists on unstintingly concentrated attention to understand the magnitude of the event and defies the possibility of such attention by its hop-scotch structure because of the very dimension of the event.

That Vonnegut could achieve the kind of intimate and casual, serious and comic, narrative tone in relating the story of Dresden and the story of his confrontation with the story of Dresden is in large part due to his style. In part, it is a style he developed as a newspaper reporter and especially as a police reporter in Chicago after the war. It is a variation on the spare, declarative style that Ernest Hemingway learned from Gertrude Stein and made famous as his own. It allows cynicism and tenderness, engagement and distance, seriousness and irony. Vonnegut's style also echoes the rhythm Mark Twain learned from the nineteenth-century American humorist and lecturer, Artemis Ward, whom he described as "pausing and hesitating, of gliding in a moment from seriousness to humor without appearing to be conscious of doing so." The style allows Vonnegut to suggest that everything is important and nothing matters, to present a belief in human betterment as absurd and yet to find as much absurdity in not attempting it.

Slaughterhouse-Five is regarded not only as one of Vonnegut's greatest achievement as a novelist but also as a book which redefined the kind of work he did. Before it, he was thought of as a science-fiction writer. With *Slaughterhouse-Five*, which incorporated characters and contrivances from his earlier books, Vonnegut became known as a serious novelist who used science-fiction elements in his books. The science-fiction elements allow Vonnegut to suggest an alternative reality governed by other laws of physics which differ from those understood to govern the phenomena of time and space on earth. Behind Vonnegut's science-fiction lie the stories of his friend, the science-fiction writer Theodore Sturgeon, who is the basis for the science-fiction author Kilgore Trout whose books strongly affect Billy Pilgrim in *Slaughterhouse-Five*.

Structurally, the novel imitates the temporal discontinuity and multi-dimensionality of Billy's consciousness and his world. At the time of the novel's publication (1969), the kind of narrative which violated the authority of sequential coherence and three-dimensional reality which *Slaughterhouse-Five* offers was becoming familiar through the wide use of consciousness altering drugs like LSD. Before that, even stream of consciousness novels like James Joyce's *Ulysses* accepted conventional reality although they explored it unconventionally. Three-dimensional Newtonian physics and clock time were understood to be the proper mappings for the events of the world. They still are, although space exploration and complex computer theory and technology as well as serious scientific investigation of parallel universes have weakened their place as the only model of reality. The practice of narrative disjunction which was exceptional when the book first appeared is also much more common now and offers readers less of a challenge than it once might have. The publication of *Slaughterhouse-Five* came just at a time when the idea of narrative order, of sequence, of the integrity of genres and individual experiences was beginning to break down and what is called a post-modern sensibility in literature, music, film, and art was yoking together in one-work elements which had until then seemed mutually exclusive.

List of Characters

Billy Pilgrim, the hero of *Slaughterhouse-Five*, was made prisoner of war by the Germans during the Second World War and taken to Dresden where he witnessed the Allied firebombing and destruction of the city. He has become "unstuck in time" and can shuttle between the experiences of his life, not bound to the linear movement of time. He has also been kidnapped by outer-space creatures from the planet Tralfamadore where he lives in a sort of geodesic dome and is displayed in a zoo.

Kurt Vonnegut appears as himself in chapter 1, in the last chapter, and sporadically throughout the book. He was imprisoned in Dresden during the bombing, witnessed it, and is obsessed with the need to write about it and say what he saw.

Bernard V. O'Hare is a war buddy of Vonnegut's, who Vonnegut visits as he tries to conduct research on the firebombing of Dresden. O'Hare is not a fictional character and therefore helps ground the work in reality.

Mary O' Hare is Bernard's wife and works as a nurse. She reflects that wars are fought by babies but written about as if they were romantic acts of mature men. She scolds Vonnegut, presuming his book will glorify war, and he promises not to and dedicates *Slaughterhouse-Five* to her.

Roland Weary is an American soldier behind enemy lines with Billy Pilgrim and is taken prisoner by the Germans along with him. He is a bully who first saves Billy's life and then tries to kill him. He is fascinated by torture devices and knives. He imagines himself playing a heroic role in the war and he dies in a boxcar on the way to the prison camp in Dresden.

Paul Lazzaro is another of Billy's war companions and a fellow prisoner. He is a vicious small time hood, a thief and a murderer, and he promises to avenge Weary's death.

Edgar Derby is another prisoner of war with Billy in Dresden. Derby is in his forties, he pulled political strings to get into the army, and he is motivated to fight by noble ideas of traditional American values like freedom, equality, and democracy. He is shot by a firing squad for taking a teapot as a souvenir from the ruins of Dresden.

Wild Bob is an army colonel who, like Roland Weary, imagines himself a valiant leader of men at war, although, in reality his entire company of forty-five hundred men was slaughtered.

Howard W. Campbell Jr. is the main character in an earlier novel, *Mother Night*, by Vonnegut. He is an American who seems to be working for the Nazi establishment as a propagandist, and that is his role in *Slaughterhouse-Five*. In *Mother Night*, it is more complicated. He is actually an American double agent sending secrets to American intelligence officers through his propaganda broadcasts.

Eliot Rosewater is also a character from another Vonnegut novel, *God Bless You, Mr. Rosewater.* In *Slaughterhouse-Five* he appears as a patient in the hospital bed next to Billy's after Billy has signed himself in because he felt he was going crazy three years after the war. Rosewater has a stash of Kilgore Trout science-fiction novels under his bed and introduces Billy to his work.

Kilgore Trout is a science-fiction writer modeled on the actual science-fiction writer and Vonnegut's friend, Theodore Sturgeon. He is a neighbor of Billy's. His books do not sell and he works as the supervisor to newspaper delivery boys. Billy's science-fiction adventures reflect events in Trout's books, which Billy has read and forgotten afterwards that he has.

Valencia Merble, Billy's wife, is described as a large woman who feared no man would ever marry her. Although Billy does not love her, their marriage is placid. He treats her with kindness and affection, and she is devoted to him.

Robert Pilgrim, Billy's son, has trouble in high school but straightens out as a Green Beret in Vietnam.

Barbara Pilgrim, Billy's daughter, marries an optometrist and enjoys her power over her father when she scolds him for believing that he has been to Tralfamadore and for appearing to be unable to take care of himself.

Montana Wildhack, formerly a movie glamour girl, has been captured by Tralfamadorians and put in the zoo-cage-home on the planet Tralfamadore with Billy to be his mate.

Professor Bertram Copeland Rumfoord is a Harvard professor and the "official" Historian of the United States Air Force. He is in the hospital bed next to Billy when Billy is hospitalized after a plane crash in Vermont. Rumfoord defends the bombing of Dresden.

Tralfamadorians are outer-space creatures who abduct Billy and look like toilet plungers. They have a hand at their top. An eye is in the hand and it can take in a range, as the hand turns, and of three hundred and sixty degrees. They have the ability to see in all directions of time, too.

Summary and Analysis

We doctors know a hopeless case.
There's a helluva good universe next door.
Let's go.
—e.e.cummings

i. Continuity and Discontinuity

The work of a novelist is not *only* to tell a story. Novelists show how stories *are told*. They show what makes something a story. They show how the world is shaped, how it is organized, how it is understood, for the way experience is organized and understood *is* a story. Novelists chart and shape our consciousness. They teach us ways to construe and to construct reality. Novelists define the nature of the world we perceive and instruct us in the ways of perceiving it. They can do this because reality is not something which exists independent of us and our perception. It exists, in large measure, because of or through us. It is defined by the way we view and compose it, by the way we understand and interpret it. And that is precisely what novelists do. They interpret reality; they view, define, and compose reality. They confirm or challenge their era's perceptions of how the world is seen and understood.

Perceiving reality is a psychological process. The story a novel tells, thus, is the story of the psychological condition of the person who tells the story, it is the story of the narrator's relation to and feeling about the surrounding world, and it is the story of how the world is composed as well as of the events recounted, the characters introduced, and the settings evoked. Perhaps the model of a narrator is Henry Fielding (1707–1754) in *Tom Jones* (1749). At the beginning of each of the novel's eighteen books, there is an introductory chapter in which Fielding, as it were, pulls his chair in front of the curtain and talks to the reader in his own person, explaining the way he has put the story together and rendering aesthetic and moral observations and judgments which essentially confirm the harmony between the world he constructs and the society to which he offers it. This harmony exists despite the variations in appetites, values, opinions, and morality that can be found among his characters or his readers. Even a story teller who seems to be discretely removed from the story being told reveals something. Such narrators—Jane Austen (1775–1817) or George Eliot (1819–1880), for example—are fundamentally in harmony with, even when commenting upon the foibles of, their society; they accept its values, rules, and formulas. Narrators more present in their works than Austen or Eliot— Charles Dickens (1812–1870) or Leo Tolstoy (1828–1910), for example—color the novel with their critical, religious, and ethical sensibilities, endowing it with their values, sentiments, outrages, and distastes. Nevertheless, neither Dickens nor Tolstoy intrudes upon his story except when he comes forward as a teacher of morality or a philosopher of history. They may—they do—challenge certain individual or institutional values, sentiments, attitudes and practices of the English during the reign of Queen Victoria, or of Russia under the rule of the Tsars, or of humankind in general, but they do not challenge the fundamental vision of how the world exists and is comprehended. Critical as they are, still they are in accord with the physics of the world they present. They do not challenge the laws of time and space. They accept the common perception of the world and the common view of heaven, too. They do not challenge the commonly perceived nature of reality or eternity but certain values and institutions. Henry James (1843–1916), invisible as he is as a narrator, nevertheless by removing himself, bent the narrative to reflect not a broad authorial and all-knowing view but the particular and skewed point of view of one character or another, calling, thus, the very idea of narrative certainty, the authority of the senses, and truth itself into question. James Joyce, difficult and obscure as he can be, wrote with the aim of revealing the true landscape of the mind as it registered the phenomena it experienced in a world of unquestioned reality.

In *Slaughterhouse-Five*,[1] Kurt Vonnegut attacks the nature of reality itself, challenging the accepted notions of time, space, and eternity. Through a series of vignettes, *Slaughterhouse-Five* begins by showing the mental state of the narrator of the book and the spiritual condition of the time in which the narrator lives. The narrator, who very closely resembles the author, Vonnegut, himself—as does his proxy, Billy Pilgrim, the hero of his story—is unsettled, even traumatized. After more than fifteen years, he is still unable to forget the Allied bombing of Dresden towards the very end of World War Two in February 1945. He experienced it first hand as a prisoner of war and ever since he has been trying to write a book about it and cannot. Adding to his disquiet, the present day world he inhabits is itself still riddled with brutality, war, and violence. Against that background, daily life is defined by a series of numbing routines inside a devitalized and mechanized consumer society. The narrator is nearly anesthetized, unable to get near enough to the memory that is nevertheless gnawing at him in order for him to take hold of it and to loosen its grip upon him. That becomes the condition of his hero, too.

In order to write of the trauma of Dresden, in order for life to make sense to him and in order not to feel hopeless in a meaningless world which makes people powerless, using elements usually found in science-fiction literature, the narrator cobbles together an imaginary world, the planet Tralfamadore, that is presented as real in which a catastrophic event like the bombing of Dresden can occur without destroying the foundations of the world or the stability of the mind or the integrity of the emotions. He invents a world governed by a different physics, therefore, from the one commonly accepted. In *Slaughterhouse-Five*, Vonnegut envisions a world which can accommodate and then neutralize catastrophes like the firebombing of Dresden and, in fact, can soothe all the pain and confusion that result from war, brutality, destruction, and death.

The post-war, post-Dresden world the narrator inhabits in **chapter 1** of *Slaughterhouse-Five* is a world that is not solid, grounded, predictable, or stable. Responses to it cannot be clear and certain. Interruption and disjunction, not continuity and connection, characterize experience. And although the Second World War ended more than twenty years before the time in which narrator is writing, the Vietnam War has replaced it with new uncontrollable horrors. Sudden, out-of-control, meaningless change is the rule, not sense and steadiness. Brutality rules in the place of reason. Vonnegut mirrors the discontinuity of the world by the way he tells the story. His narration is not sequential. It jumps around in time and through space. Events are not presented in linear order. Transitions are abrupt; narrative sections, small, only several paragraphs long. Sentences are usually short, and sentence structure is simple.

In **chapter 1**, fragments of obscene doggerel and profound poetry flood the narrator's mind. He recalls the job as police reporter he held after the war. There is a quick scene in a taxi cab in East Germany with a cab driver who had been a prisoner of the Americans during the war and whose mother was "incinerated" (1) in Dresden. Now he finds life comfortable enough in East Germany. Vonnegut quotes from books about Dresden and about the Children's Crusade of the middle ages. He describes waterfalls and late night alcohol binges. He is at the kitchen table of a friend's house. He tells the reader the first and last lines of the book. A verse about a Wisconsin worker circles endlessly in his mind. The narrator establishes himself as the center of his tale and he establishes the credibility of his narrative by the extent of his intimate self-revelation.

What makes Billy Pilgrim unique—an optometrist who, like Vonnegut was a prisoner-of-war in Dresden at the time it was bombed and who is the narrator's surrogate—the book's hero—is that he has adapted perfectly to a world in which he is adrift without the ability to influence anything and events have no reasonable continuity to them. He lives according to laws of space and time different from the ones which govern the Earth. Adrift in a world incoherent and discontinuous, Billy Pilgrim adapts to it unconsciously, without effort conforms himself to it. His story begins in **chapter 2** with the information that he "has come unstuck in time." (17) Instead of in the confusing and fragmented war-shocked world that tosses him about so violently that he loses all sense of orientation, Billy lives in the four dimensional, space-time physics of a science-fiction novel and effortlessly goes from here to there and from now to then. His world is governed by a physics which takes the sting, finality, and fatality out of any event, no matter how awful. The world Billy enters permits him to see beyond the limited laws of the Earth's three dimensional reality—and Vonnegut presents it as if it were real. The book is not written as a case history where the setting from the outset is presented and recognized as a character's delusion but as a science-fiction story in which such a setting as the planet Tralfamadore is perfectly plausible because of the conventions of the genre.

ii. Making the Frame

Slaughterhouse-Five is a story within a story. Its context is established in an introductory chapter and by a few paragraphs in the concluding chapter. **Chapter 1** begins with an assurance by the author-narrator that "All this happened," as if guaranteeing the integrity of a work so full of fantasy. A wary reader immediately is put on guard by the assurance. Suspicion that it may not be so is confirmed by the three words which finish the sentence: "more or less." In these six words, Vonnegut introduces the basic instability the novel is founded on, grows out of, describes, and celebrates. The narrator continues to explain that many of the specific facts of the novel are true: "One guy I knew really was shot in Dresden...for taking a teapot.... Another...did threaten to have his enemy killed by hired gunmen after the war....I really did go back to Dresden with Guggenheim money." (1)

Vonnegut recounts these pieces of the story casually in the same off-hand manner that characterizes the entire novel. Nevertheless, they are essential parts of the story. In a more conventionally structured narrative, the assassination of Billy Pilgrim by a gunman hired by Paul Lazzaro or the execution of Earl Derby for taking a teapot from the ruins of Dresden after the bombing would constitute climaxes to complex plots or penetrating character studies, arrived at, built up to, so that they might offer maximum dramatic, ironic, or emotion-laden impact. Here Vonnegut tosses them off. And he mentions them repeatedly throughout the narrative until they become leitmotivs, recurring phrases—like the expressions, "And so on," or "So it goes," which follows every account of a death the way the word "Amen" follows every blessing uttered during a religious service. Repetition makes these events so familiar to the reader that the narrator seems to be telling a story the reader already knows. This is rhetorically useful in a story that is fantastic if taken literally. It helps the reader suspend disbelief. Making events familiar before they are fully narrated reflects, moreover, the time sense of the novel. Everything that happens has happened already and will happen again and again.

Narrative repetition drains suspense from the story and frustrates linearity. Things don't develop. They keep coming back. Without linearity, there is no sense of history. History is based on the perception that one thing follows another in an orderly progression from past through present to future. In *Slaughterhouse-Five*, the non-linear narrative creates the impression that everything is laid out before us to experience at once, that all moments are simultaneous, and, therefore, that everything exists outside of time and that time, consequently, does not exist. This is the way experience is structured on the planet Tralfamadore, where Billy's alien captors take him. The Tralfamadorian sense of time, or of un-time, negates death, pain, and loss. Death is not a culminating event but a fixed and recurring event among many fixed and recurring events all perceived simultaneously. Death is not the last event on a string of time. Tralfamadorians, Vonnegut reports at the beginning of **chapter 5**, do not see the universe as "a lot of bright little dots." They "see where each star has been and where it is going, so that the heavens are filled with rarefied, luminous spaghetti." (63) Since all time can be seen at once, no one moment of time has any greater strength than any other moment of time. There is no distinction between "now" and "then." Neither exists.

Perhaps the most significant of the several episodes Vonnegut relates in **chapter 1** as he is setting the context for the main story of *Slaughterhouse-Five* is his encounter with Mary O'Hare, the wife of his old war buddy in Dresden

Bernard V. O'Hare. The narrator telephones Bernard O'Hare late one night, drunk. He makes an appointment to visit him so that they can sit around and swap stories for the Dresden novel he is working on, the book which becomes *Slaughterhouse-Five*. Vonnegut takes his daughter and her friend with him to O'Hare's. After the children go upstairs to play with the O'Hare children and Vonnegut prepares to sit down with Bernard to reminisce, he realizes that O'Hare's wife is fuming with suppressed anger at him. When Mary can hold it in no longer she tells him,

> You were just babies in the war....But you're not going to write it that way....You'll pretend you were men instead of babies, and you'll be played in the movies by Frank Sinatra and John Wayne or some of those other glamorous, war-loving, dirty old men. And war will look just wonderful, so we'll have a lot more of them. And they'll be fought by babies....

Vonnegut reports that he answered her like this, "I held up my right hand and I made her a promise: 'Mary,' I said, '...I give you my word of honor: there won't be a part in it for Frank Sinatra or John Wayne.'" (11) He promises to look at war differently from how it is usually regarded, to examine it under a lens that does not romanticize or glamorize it.

To do that, Vonnegut makes Billy Pilgrim an optometrist, a doctor who fits people with corrective lenses. Rather than an active he-man movie hero, Vonnegut portrays him as a passive soul and a kind of holy fool. Vonnegut makes Billy Pilgrim a lens himself. Through him Vonnegut can show readers the effects of war on the psyche and show how traumatic experience can fashion an alternative way of seeing things, which may or may not be mad. Vonnegut presents war itself as mad: vile, absurd, and vulgar. Rather than heroic battle scenes and noble heroes, there are repulsive images of latrines and of the collection and disposal of ordure. Among the principal characters Weary and Lazarro are loathsome in their sadism. The admirable Edgar Derby upholds honorable, democratic values, and he is executed by the army for taking a souvenir teapot from the ruins of the city that has just been massacred by the military. (91)

By putting the metaphor of optometry at the center of his novel, Vonnegut offers the reader an interpretive or analytic aid for making sense of the novel. Just as Billy Pilgrim's profession is a metaphor for the novelist's task in *Slaughterhouse-Five*—the task of both is to correct faulty vision—so other elements of the story, too, like time travel and the outer-space adventure with the Tralfamadorians can be seen as metaphors. Rather than reflecting Billy's mental derangement, they satirize the necessary accommodations such events as the bombing of Dresden provoke. Through the use of science-fiction, Vonnegut talks about human psychological responses to trauma and about alternative ways of exercising human consciousness. The question of whether Billy is mad or sane does not really interest him. The quality, validity, and virtue, the inevitability of the vision he has had, because of the war, by becoming unstuck in time and visiting Tralfamadore do interest him. Vonnegut gives the hardheaded reader a chance to explain away Billy's space travel as delusion. He reports that Billy has been hospitalized for several mental breakdowns and that he is a great fan of the science-fiction writing of his neighbor, Kilgore Trout. He even meets Trout in **chapter 8**. Trout's stories parallel Billy's adventures. Nevertheless, Vonnegut does not discredit the vision by doing so. That he imagines telling Billy's story as a science-fiction tale rather than a case history insures that. In **chapter 2**, moreover, the narrator, in his own voice, notes, regarding a "delightful hallucination" Billy had of skating over a ballroom floor in white socks to great cheers, that "this wasn't time travel. It had never happened, never would happen. It was the craziness of a dying young man with his shoes full of snow."(35) Noting that this experience was crazy gives that much more credibility to others not so labeled.

iii. Seeing the Lenses

Vonnegut begins **chapter 2** of *Slaughterhouse-Five* with a description of Billy Pilgrim's condition from Billy's point of view. He presents it as a fact of experience rather than as a symptom of mental disease.

> Billy Pilgrim has come unstuck in time. [He] has gone to sleep a senile widower and awakened on his wedding day. He has walked through a door in 1955 and come out another one in 1941. He has gone back through that door to find himself in 1963. He has seen his birth and death many times...and pays random visits to all the events in between. (17)

This is a synopsis of the action and a blueprint of the structure of *Slaughterhouse-Five* as well as an account of Billy Pilgrim's situation. The action is essentially a journey through shifting timescapes. Time itself is like a house with many rooms one may enter and leave at random. Mirroring Billy's experience, the novel is a kind of merry-go-round. Scenes, events, and images keep reappearing. Rather than offering the reader a rollercoaster ride of suspense and release through time and space as emerging situations are developed, *Slaughterhouse-Five* goes round and round through a circle of repetitions continually turning on events recognizably familiar. Images that recall each other, likewise, return. The railroad tracks in Dresden, called "the steel spaghetti of the railroad yard" (108) in **chapter 6** suggest the "luminous spaghetti"(63) of the stars in **chapter 5**. Independent events, too, recapitulate each other. Thrown into the war just as he was thrown into a swimming pool as a baby, in both cases it was a matter of sink or swim for Billy Pilgrim. In both cases, sinking was the more attractive option, but in both cases he was rescued. The resonance of one event in another, of one image in another, rather than linear development leading from situation to situation, is the mark of continuity and structural integrity both in the story and in the style of *Slaughterhouse-Five*.

As if to get it out of the way, Vonnegut relates the story of *Slaughterhouse-Five* in a few paragraphs in linear fashion. He starts with Billy Pilgrim's birth in 1922—the year of Vonnegut's birth—and goes through to the last years of his life as a widower and a proselytizer "devoting himself to a calling much higher than mere business." (21). Billy was "the only child of a barber….He was funny looking….He graduated…in the upper third of his [high school] class." Afterwards, he went to optometry school "for one semester before being drafted for military service in the Second World War. His father died in a hunting accident during the war." Billy served in the infantry in Europe and "was taken prisoner by the Germans." He went back to optometry school in 1945 after being discharged from the army. He became engaged to the daughter of the founder and owner of the school in his senior year "and then suffered a mild nervous collapse." Billy "was treated in a veteran's hospital…given shock treatments and released. He married," was set up in a lucrative business as an optometrist by his father-in-law, "became rich….had two children." His daughter, Barbara, married an optometrist and his son, Robert, "had a lot of trouble in high school, but then he joined the famous Green Berets….straightened out…and fought in Vietnam." (17–18) In 1968, the biographical sketch continues, Billy was the sole survivor of a plane crash. His wife, driving to visit him at the hospital where he was recovering from head injuries, died in the car of carbon monoxide poisoning.

In several more short paragraphs, Vonnegut finishes the sketch of Billy's life, tells how Billy, once home from the hospital, decided to go to New York, got on an all-night radio talk show and told how he had been kidnapped by aliens, taken to the planet Tralfamadore, and put on display there along with a Hollywood movie star, Montana Wildhack, who had been abducted to be his mate. When several of his neighbors in his home town, Illium, New York, heard the broadcast, they were scandalized, as they were later when Billy wrote a letter to the editor recounting his experience. In their minds, he had gone crazy. Vonnegut's synopsis, however, establishes Billy's view of things as the novel's. Significantly he does not include in this narrative string that Billy read Kilgore Trout's science-fiction novels while he was in the hospital, after his mental breakdown, in 1948 and then forgot he had read them. Doing so would break the narrative ambiguity and take away the strong presence Tralfamadore has as an experience *for the reader*. With the scene of his daughter, Barbara, reproaching Billy for embarrassing her and her husband, Vonnegut brings the story of Billy's life up to the present. But the point of *Slaughterhouse-Five* is that there is no present. Vonnegut simply ends that narrative episode of the novel and shifts to a presentation of the Tralfamadorian philosophy, which Billy comes to advance because "so many...souls" on earth "were lost and wretched," and he was "prescribing corrective lenses for Earthling souls." (21) In one of his letters to the local newspaper, Billy writes,

> The most important thing I learned on Tralfamadore was that when a person dies he only *appears* to die. He is still very much alive in the past....All moments, past, present, and future, always have existed, always will exist. The Tralfamadorians can look at all the different moments just the way we can look at a stretch of the Rocky Mountains....They can see how permanent all the moments are, and they can look at any moment that interests them. It is an illusion we have on Earth that one moment follows another one like beads on a string, and once that moment is gone it is gone forever. (19)

The Tralfamadorian gospel makes it seem reasonable to be unstuck in time. Time is illusory and, consequently, so is loss. In a universe that exists outside of time, there is nothing that can cease to be. Psychologically, whether Tralfamadore is "real" in the novel or a delusion in Billy's mind, it and its belief system as well as the process of coming unstuck in time rise out of and serve to compensate for the traumatic experience of the firebombing of Dresden. That event is presented inside the frame of Billy's misadventures in the war and in the light of the Tralfamadorian consciousness he brings to everything. Vonnegut writes, in fact, that because "Billy had seen the greatest massacre in European history, which was the firebombing of Dresden," he tried "to reinvent [himself] and [his] universe." (73) Rather than being a version of madness, it seems, Billy's vision is a strategy to prevent madness. To accept either the reasonableness or the finality of the bombing of Dresden and the implications of such actions with regard to humanity itself and to the nature of existence, according to *Slaughterhouse-Five*, would be to bring on madness for that very reality is unhinged. To re-construe reality and enter an alternate world also appears to be madness. When war is the reality, it seems that every option one has to respond to it must be tinged with madness. But Tralfamadorian metaphysics offers the readjustment of perception necessitated by the reality of Dresden to keep a kind of sanity through madness. If you're going to have events like Dresden, Vonnegut seems to say, it would make more sense to have them in a Tralfamadorian universe than in one like ours. A crazy response to a crazy situation makes sense.

iv. Billy Pilgrim in the War

Vonnegut begins his account of Billy Pilgrim in the war, in **chapter 2**, by jumping from a scene in which his daughter, Barbara, is scolding Billy for what to her is his embarrassing Tralfamadorian nonsense to a scene in South Carolina in 1944, when Billy, a chaplain's assistant, experienced the uncanny encounter of what is and of what is imagined. In a mock, practice air attack, a congregation of fifty soldiers "had been theoretically spotted from the air by a theoretical enemy. They were all theoretically dead." But the bizarre reality, as Billy perceived it was that "[t]he theoretical corpses laughed and ate a hearty noontime meal;" (23) that, depending upon how you thought about them, they could be either dead or alive and thus were dead and alive at the same time.

Soon after this epiphany, Billy is furloughed because of his father's death in a hunting accident. When he returns to duty, he is sent to Luxembourg to fight in the Battle of the Bulge and soon is wandering behind enemy lines with three other soldiers displaced in the battle. In his account of Billy and the three others, Vonnegut keeps his promise to Mary O'Hare, presenting war as neither heroic nor romantic. With Billy, who "didn't look like a soldier at all," but "like a filthy flamingo," are two scouts and Roland Weary. Weary is "clumsy and dense…stupid and fat and mean, and smelled like bacon no matter how much he washed." He is eighteen. In school, "he would find someone who was even more unpopular than himself, and he would horse around with [him] for a while, pretending to be friendly. And then he would find some pretext for beating the shit out of him." (23, 25) He is fascinated by guns and knives and torture instruments, and he carries an obscene picture of a woman and a Shetland pony. Vonnegut describes him as "murderous." This wretched band wander through the snow without food or maps or proper shoes. Billy wants only to surrender to the inertia of death, but Weary keeps saving his life and pulling him along until he is ready to kill him. As he is about to deliver fatal kicks to Billy's spinal column, the two are caught and taken prisoners by a German patrol. Thus, in the convoluted ironic reality of *Slaughterhouse-Five*, the comrade who has been saving Billy is his near assassin, and the enemy who was taking shots at him from a distance, saves his life.

Roland Weary is not only an unappealing character designed to highlight brutal and disgusting aspects of war. He is also the purveyor of the point of view Vonnegut has pledged to Mary O'Hare not to celebrate in his novel, and, indeed, Vonnegut uses Roland Weary to mock and discredit it. Weary goes through the war with a counter-narrative to the author's.

Weary's version of the true war story went like this: There was a big German attack, and Weary and his antitank buddies fought like hell until everybody was killed but Weary….And then Weary tied in with two scouts, and they became close friends immediately, and they decided to fight their way back to their own lines. They were going to travel fast. They were damned if they'd surrender. They shook hands all around. They called themselves "The Three Musketeers."

But then this damn college kid, who was so weak he shouldn't even have been in the army, asked if he could come along. He didn't even have a gun or a knife. He didn't even have a helmet or a cap. He couldn't even walk right—kept bobbing up-and-down, up-and-down, driving everybody crazy, giving their position away. He was pitiful. The Three Musketeers pushed and carried and dragged the college kid all the way back to their own lines, Weary's story went. (30)

Another counter-narrative, similar to Roland Weary's appears in **chapter 3**. The dying American colonel from Wyoming, who fancies himself as "Wild Bob," whose entire regiment of forty-five hundred men has been killed, "imagined he was addressing his troops for the last time and told them they had nothing to be ashamed of, that there were dead Germans all over the battlefield who wished to God that they had never heard of the Four-fifty-first" (49) regiment. He invites his whole outfit, in his oration, to a regimental barbecue and reunion at his home in Cody, Wyoming, after the war. As in the case of Roland Weary's counter-narrative, Vonnegut is mocking the posturing of heroes in stories which glorify war. Additionally, he not only presents the true face of war by showing the discrepancy between how those who fight it think of it and how it really is but he also shows how perceived reality, whether Billy's Tralfamadore or Weary's war, can be a mental, even a fictional construction.

Billy's counter-narrative, which is the authoritative narrative of the book, whether or not it is "true" and "sane," also begins in the war. It is not, like Weary's or Wild Bob's, a narrative which denies the actuality of the war with a clichéd John-Wayne-movie version of male heroism, bonding, and sacrifice. Billy's is a transcendental narrative that does not alter the reality of his war experience but of the very nature of the universe it is a part of so that the experience can be made endurable. Thus Billy is in the war and somewhere else simultaneously. He lives in his mind, and the landscape of his mind is as real as the topography of the battlefield.

During the war "Billy first came unstuck in time." He experienced a number of other events in his life, was physically present at them as he "was leaning against a tree with his eyes closed" in the German forest. First, "his attention began to swing grandly through the full arc of his life, passing into death, which was violet light….And then Billy swung into life again and stopped. He was a little boy taking a shower with his hairy father at the Illium Y.M.C.A." He smelled the "chlorine from the pool next door." He experienced terror. "His father had said Billy was going to learn by the method of sink-or-swim." (31) When his father then threw him into the pool, Billy sank to the bottom and began to die. But then he sensed that someone was rescuing him.

Before the narrative returns to Germany in 1944, when Billy is being shaken awake by Roland Weary, Billy travels through a number of other-time experiences. He visits his "decrepit mother at…an old people's home." (32) In the waiting room, Billy, a mental and spiritual deserter, reads a book about the execution of an American soldier in front of a firing squad for desertion and cowardice. He attends a banquet for his son's Little League baseball team. He is caught cheating on his wife while he is drunk during a party. And he searches for the steering wheel of his car, afterwards, still drunk, but cannot find it because he is sitting in the back seat. The image is a metaphor for his rudderless condition.

These episodes do not advance the story or develop the plot. They are an accumulation of vignettes that parallel, contrast with, or comment upon Billy's experience in the war. They illuminate aspects of his character and his mental condition. Experienced as time travel, and presented from Billy's point of view, these episodes can also be understood as a flood of associated memories and fantasies into which Billy retreats from the battlefield or which block his memory of the war. Like memories, fantasies, or dreams, they are the events of a life that have been liberated from the continuum of time and the boundaries of space. They endlessly and randomly recur, reflect and recall each other. Existing like memories and dreams in their own dimensions they both shield Billy from a traumatic experience and keep referring to it. Since Vonnegut does not present Billy's mental experience clinically, moreover, but in terms of the conventions of a science-fiction story, readers can enter those dimensions and experience them as narrative reality.

v. Juxtaposition

Without a sequential narrative, and without the operation of cause and effect which furthers the development of a plot, the relation the parts of a story have to each other tends to get lost unless another organizing element can be found. In *Slaughterhouse-Five*, that element is juxtaposition. The way one vignette, one image, one nugget of the story reflects, connects to, and is played off the others enhances the meaning, depth or dimension of each element. By the contrast and association of small sections, Vonnegut gives the novel its unity and makes the meaning it develops an experience rather than just an assertion.

Since the pieces are read in relation to each other, they provide commentary on each other and give each other depth. This kind of construction signals that the novel is concerned with developing ideas about the events it is recounting more than with telling a story, generating drama, or developing and probing human character. Even Billy Pilgrim, like the other characters in *Slaughterhouse-Five*, is, after all, a flat character, entirely defined as his tale begins. He does not grow or change throughout the course of the novel. Readers do not learn about him but about varieties of perceiving, reacting, and experiencing. He simply functions according to the way his author designed him. Quite near the end of the novel, in fact, at the beginning of **chapter 8**, Vonnegut says as much. "There are almost no characters in this story, and almost no dramatic confrontations." (119) It is a novel about the psychic effects of war and brutality on systems of human perception, not about people or adventures.

In order to get a sense of how *Slaughterhouse-Five* is constructed, and how Vonnegut achieves a sense of unity and conveys meaning, look at four vignettes which follow one another in **chapter 3**. The first is set at the time the novel was actually published, during the late 1960s, at the height of the Vietnam War. Billy is listening to a Major in the Marines deliver a speech supporting the war and advocating "bombing North Vietnam back into the stone age" at a Lions Club meeting in Illium. The second vignette describes a setting. The Alcoholics Anonymous prayer—"God grant me the serenity to accept the things I cannot change, courage to change the things I can, and wisdom always to tell the difference"—hangs, framed, in Billy's office. The third vignette returns to the Lions Club meeting and shows the Marine Major after his talk telling Billy that "the Green Berets were doing a great job, and that he should be proud of his son." Billy answers, "I *am*. I certainly *am*." The fourth vignette shows Billy at home taking a nap, and 'find[ing] himself weeping," as he did "every so often." (44)

Taken together these four scenes suggest that Billy Pilgrim's affectlessness and resignation are symptomatic of repressed pain rather than healthy adjustments. Additionally, they offer an implicit condemnation of the Vietnam War. The Major's position is not presented as a caricature—there really were people who were saying just such things. He represents a position that has been clearly repudiated in the first chapter of the novel, in Vonnegut's aside about the Dresden "massacre" and by the narrator's remark in **chapter 5** (73) that Billy was trying to reinvent himself and his universe as a consequence of his war experience. Moreover, in a conversation Vonnegut will later relate that takes place between Billy and his Tralfamadorian captors in which Billy wonders "How the inhabitants of a whole planet can live in peace!" Billy laments,

As you know, I am from a planet that has been engaged in senseless slaughter since the beginning of time. I...have seen the bodies of schoolgirls who were boiled alive in a water tower by my own countrymen....And I have lit my way to prison at night with candles from the fat of human beings who were butchered by the brothers and fathers of those schoolgirls who were boiled. (84)

Billy's response to the Major's position, even without these and other countervailing assertions, is of especial interest because it shows how narrative works in *Slaughterhouse-Five*. The response is presented from three points of view. What Billy says to the major, that he certainly is proud, is apparently honest, or at least it is his public truth. Yet the sign in his office indicates a rather strong degree of resignation to things as they are, rather than agreement, especially because, the narrator immediately appends after presenting the prayer, "among the things Billy Pilgrim could not change were the past, the present, and the future." (44) What is left is changing himself and his way of responding to, of viewing, past, present, and future. He can postulate and escape to a world different from the one he cannot change. Billy's public acceptance of the unchangeable world, however, does not seem to have been successfully achieved. When he is by himself, when his guard is down, Billy cries quietly and without many tears. His deeper, private self knows another truth, not the Tralfamadorian philosophy but the reason it exists for him. Although he is not consciously aware of why he cries, the context of the novel suggests he is crying for himself, for the loss of his innocent integrity, for the buried pacifist conviction demanded by his experience, and because he needs to escape from his public self through fourth-dimensional and extra-terrestrial travel in order to be himself.

The narrative assumes a degree of linearity, although there are narrative jumps and interruptions, as Vonnegut charts the course of Billy's journey as a prisoner-of-war from Luxembourg to Dresden in **chapter 6**. But as in other episodes, the vignettes of his journey are not devoted to developing the story, which has already been outlined. There are no surprises. The vignettes are designed to amplify a reader's sense of experiencing what the characters experience from an absurd point of view and to create in the reader sympathy for the anti-war position of both the author and his main character. The experience of war is simultaneously meaningful and meaningless. The vignettes convey a sense of the brutality and absurdity of war and discredit conventional war narratives and their clichés, like the John Wayne movie playing in Roland Weary's imagination or the picture of the captured British prisoners who keep their upper lips stiff through personal hygiene, exercise, and hearty camaraderie.

vi. Tralfamadore

The non-linear, fragmentary structure of *Slaughterhouse-Five* reflects the fourth-dimensional reality of the Tralfamadorians who kidnap Billy Pilgrim and display him in a zoo on Tralfamadore. When, in **chapter 5**, he is in their spacecraft on the way to Tralfamadore, Billy asks his captors for something to read, and they describe what the novel is like on Tralfamadore. Tralfamadorian novels are "laid out in brief clumps of symbols separated by stars.... They are telegrams.... [E]ach clump of symbols is a brief urgent message—describing a situation, a scene." The Tralfamadorians do not read them sequentially but "all at once." Moreover, like the structure of *Slaughterhouse-Five*,

> there isn't any particular relationship between all the messages, except that the author has chosen them carefully, so that, when seen all at once, they produce an image of life that is beautiful and surprising and deep. There is no beginning, no middle, no end, no suspense, no moral, no causes, no effects. What we love in our books are the depth of many marvelous moments seen all at once. (64)

Their novels reflect their way of perceiving the world, time, and experience. *Slaughterhouse-Five* is Vonnegut's Earth-oriented version of a Tralfamadorian novel. It enables readers to construe reality, through form and through content, in a Tralfamadorian way. The connection of all moments to each other is conveyed by the way episodes and images reverberate and repeat throughout. Vonnegut calls his method in the book's long subtitle a "telegraphic schizophrenic manner." In *Slaughterhouse-Five*, Vonnegut attempts to have readers see events the way the Tralfamadorians see the stars, not as points bounded by time, but as ribbons of spaghetti swirling through time. By seeing things that way the book offers a method that can neutralize the pain of the moment, for there is no moment.

But the need for such a tranquilizing philosophy indicates the magnitude of the event precipitating it.

When he is kidnapped by the Tralfamadorians, in **chapter 4**, Billy asks, "why me?"(55) It is the echo of a question an American soldier asks of a German soldier who is beating him in **chapter 6**. And the question can expand to the great conundrums of the book, Why Dresden? and, especially, Why war and brutality? Whether from the Tralfamadorians or the German the answer to the question of why is the same, although the Tralfamadorians are more thorough and more explicit in answering: "Why *you*? Why *us* for that matter? Why *anything*? Because the moment simply *is*....We are trapped in the amber of the moment. There is no why." The German simply answers, "Vy you? Vy anybody?" (66)

The meaning varies according to the speaker. Unlike the philosophical Tralfamadorians who have discovered the secret of random inevitability and accepted it, the German is simply at a loss and angry at the apparent totalitarianism of fate. But there is a connection. In *Slaughterhouse-Five*, anger at the totalitarianism of fate is transformed into acceptance of the inevitable. Thus whether Billy is in Germany or on Tralfamadore he is in a different version of the same place undergoing different versions of the same event. Being captured by the Germans during World War II and being kidnapped by aliens from the planet Tralfamadore after the war are experiences that reflect and recapitulate each other. The science-fiction story simply puts a positive spin on the war story. Vonnegut establishes the parallel between Billy's prisoner-of-war experiences and his abduction in **chapter 4**,

Billy blacked out as he walked through gate after gate. He came to in what he thought might be a building on Tralfamadore. It was lit and lined with white tiles. It was on Earth, though. It was a delousing station through which all new prisoners had to pass.

Billy did as he was told, took off his clothes. That was the first thing they told him to do on Tralfamadore, too. (59–60)

As he is showered while his clothes are being deloused, Billy "zoomed back in time to his infancy." Another parallel transformation occurs. He "was a baby who had just been bathed by his mother." She then wraps him in a towel, carries "him into a rosy room filled with sunshine," and powders him. No matter the grim painfulness of external experience, Billy has the capacity to short circuit that experience and converts it into a sweet inner experience that overwhelms and replaces it. (60–61) Vonnegut also manages, once more, to keep his promise to Mary O'Hare by contrasting the image of a baby in the affectionate care of its mother to the images of war's brutality and alienation.

The only way to make sense of the war is to believe, as the Tralfamadorians do, that things that are must be whether they are now, have been, or will be. In a dimension where time does not exist, to know what will happen gives a person no more power to change what will happen than to know what has happened gives a person the power to change what has happened. But it does not really matter because everything, not just the thing we happen to be aware of, is always happening and we can not do anything about it. "All time is all time. It does not change. It does not lend itself to warnings or explanations. It simply *is*." (62) Billy accepts as the nature of things on Tralfamadore what he is forced to endure in war, complete helplessness, existing outside time, a sense that he is "the listless plaything of enormous forces." (119)

The important thing then becomes where you look, what image you choose to see. "Concentrate on the happy moments of … life … ignore the unhappy ones…stare only at pretty things as eternity fail[s] to go by," is the Tralfamadorian advice offered in **chapter 9**. (142) This wisdom of Tralfamadore is just the sort of doctrine someone who has been traumatized by events that render him entirely powerless might invent in order to reduce the effect of the trauma. Vonnegut's novel about Dresden is a novel about coping with the fact of the bombing of Dresden or with any other of the many terrible things that define earthly existence. Rather than being an optimistic philosophy, once it is seen for what it is, Tralfamadorian metaphysics reveals itself to be a deeply pessimistic and resigned way of coping.

vii. The Difficulty of Protesting the Bombing of Dresden

Writing an American novel condemning the bombing of Dresden is a delicate undertaking, however beautiful the city may have been and no matter how many people perished. In many people there is a first response against feeling remorse for bombing enemy territory. Vonnegut incorporates it into the book using the words of United States Air Force Lieutenant General Ira C. Eaker (an actual person, not a fictional character) written as the Preface to a book about the bombing of Dresden by an English author, David Irving:

> I find it difficult to understand Englishmen or Americans who weep about enemy civilians who were killed but who have not shed a tear for our gallant crews lost in combat with a cruel enemy ... I think it would have been well for Mr. Irving to have remembered, when he was drawing the frightful picture of the civilians killed at Dresden, that V - 1's and V -2s were at that very time falling on England, killing civilian men, women, and children indiscriminately, as they were designed and launched to do. It might be well to remember Buchenwald and Coventry, too....
>
> I deeply regret that British and U.S. bombers killed 135,000 people in the attack on Dresden, but I remember who started the last war and I regret even more the loss of more than 5,000,000 Allied lives in the necessary effort to completely defeat and utterly destroy nazism. (136–137)

Vonnegut reports in **chapter 1** that he has heard this argument when

> I happened to tell a University of Chicago professor ... about the raid as I had seen it, about the book I would write.... And he told me about the concentration camps, and about how the Germans had made soap and candles out of the fat of dead Jews and so on.

Vonnegut does not offer an intellectual refutation. He figuratively shrugs his shoulders, not dismissing objection but indicating that the latitude of grief and blame in war is without boundary: acts of violence generate each other. He reports, "All I could say was, "I know, I know. I *know*." (6–7) Each violation of humanity tends to negate or excuse another such violation. But *Slaughterhouse-Five* does not lessen the horror or violate the memory of Buchenwald and Coventry. It amplifies them. Vonnegut takes the risk of considering all people as human and all horror as horrible no matter who is its object, no matter what the apparent justification.

viii. Billy's Companions During the War

The three figures who share Billy's war adventures are types, almost caricatures, rather than characters. Roland Weary, who lived inside the false daydream of war's glamour, camaraderie, and adventure and who was eerily fond of knives and instruments of torture, died in a boxcar transport on the way to Dresden, but he transferred his malevolent influence to another of Billy's companions-in-war, Paul Lazzaro, who had enough malignancy of his own. Lazzaro is the "guy" Vonnegut refers to in **chapter 1** who "really did threaten to have his personal enemies killed by a hired gunman after the war." (1) Lazarro was "a car thief from Illinois....his skin was disgusting." He "was polka-dotted with dime-sized scars" and "boils." (60) In the boxcar, before he died, Weary told Lazzaro and everyone else, although it was only a fabrication, a part of the war story he was telling himself, that Billy Pilgrim was responsible for his death, and made Lazzaro promise to avenge him. Lazzaro does, and on February 13, 1976, thirty-one years to the day after the bombing of Dresden, a gunman working for him assassinates Billy in Chicago. Lazarro is like the blocked memory of the bombing of Dresden that trails Billy and will one day explode inside him.

Although Lazarro's viciousness illustrates that things are inevitably the way they are and often rotten, he serves a purpose in *Slaughterhouse-Five* beyond being another bad experience of war and the incarnation of Billy's angel of death. In the terms of the story, after all, Billy's death has very little importance and in terms of its plot has hardly any dramatic weight. The most significant thing about it, in fact, is that it is of no concern to Billy himself. Nor is Lazzaro significant because he demonstrates the possible depths of human depravity. What earns Lazzaro a place in the story is his response to the bombing of Dresden given *his* depravity.

Billy first encountered Lazzaro in a German prison hospital. Watching an obscene rendition of the Cinderella story put on by the British prisoners to welcome and entertain the newly arrived Americans, Billy began laughing at a particularly vulgar couplet and "went on shrieking until he was carried out of the shed and into another, where the hospital was." In the hospital shed Billy was "put to bed and tied down, and given a shot of morphine." (71) Lazarro was brought to the hospital later the same night with a broken arm because he had been "caught stealing cigarettes from under the pillow of an Englishman." Half in his sleep, the Englishman "had broken Lazzaro's right arm and knocked him unconscious." (92) Chewing on his anger at the Englishman, Lazzaro revealed the depths of his nastiness by describing the way he once took revenge—"the sweetest thing there is," he says—on a dog that bit him:

I got me some steak, and I got me the spring out of a clock. I cut that spring up in little pieces. I put points on the ends of the pieces. They were sharp as razor blades. I stuck 'em into the steak—way inside. And I went past where they had the dog tied up. He wanted to bite me again. I said to him,
'Come on, doggie—let's be friends. Let's not be enemies any more. I'm not mad"....I threw him the steak. He swallowed it in one big gulp. I waited around for ten minutes....Blood started coming out of his mouth. He started crying, and he rolled on the ground, as though the knives were on the outside of him instead of on the inside of him. Then he tried to bite out his own insides, I laughed and I said to him, "You got the right idea now.

Tear your own guts out, boy. That's *me* in there with all those knives."

But "when Dresden was destroyed later on," Vonnegut reports

Lazzaro did not exult. He didn't have anything against the Germans, he said. Also, he said he liked to take his enemies one at a time. He was proud of never having hurt an innocent bystander. "Nobody ever got it from Lazzaro," he said, "who didn't have it coming." (101)

The street ethics of a small-time, vicious, and repulsive two-bit thug have more to recommend them, Vonnegut suggests, than the morality of war.

When Billy was tied to his bed and sedated, Edgar Derby watched over him and read Stephen Crane's anguished portrayal of the American Civil War, *The Red Badge of Courage* to him. Derby is Lazzaro's moral opposite. Thematically, however, his role is the same: to discredit war. Derby is the noble martyr of the book, not Billy. Billy is the victim hero of the book. He transcends victimization through his discovery of Tralfamadore and time travel. Battered by reality, he remains untouched by it, nevertheless. He is a pilgrim who ventures into new territory. Derby is fixed in an inescapable three-dimensional reality and a believer in old-fashioned values. He is undermined and defeated by the irony of war's injustice.

In contrast to Lazzaro, who was the "worst body" in the war, Derby was "one of the best bodies." A high school teacher before he enlisted, he was older than the others, forty-four, and "had pulled political wires to get into the army." (60) Unlike Lazzaro and Weary, who are brutes, and even unlike Billy, who is "out of it," Derby is an idealist. He defends the traditional American values he believed were the principles guiding American involvement in the war. When Howard W. Campbell, "an American who had become a Nazi," (118) visits the American war prisoners in order to enlist them in his "Free America Corps," to fight for the Germans against the Russians, Campbell spoke movingly of the American form of government with freedom and justice and opportunities and fair play for all. He said there wasn't a man who wouldn't gladly die for those ideals.

He spoke of the brotherhood between the American and the Russian people, and how those two nations were going to crush the disease of Nazism. (119–120)

Vonnegut's melancholy and laconic summary of his fate comes in the last chapter, **chapter 10**, six paragraphs from the end. "The poor old high school teacher, Edgar Derby, was caught with a teapot he had taken from the catacombs. He was arrested for plundering. He was tried and shot." (157) Nothing more said, except the usual "So it goes." The news is not a surprise. Vonnegut has been announcing it since the first paragraph of the book. Yet here it stands quietly and ironic in the context of the awful destruction of Dresden with outraged dignity as an indictment of war.

ix. Reconstructing Billy's Story

Had Vonnegut told the story of *Slaughterhouse-Five* in a straightforward way, it would have read like a case history: Traumatized by a he-man father who tossed him into a swimming pool when he was a baby, Billy grew up to be a rather passive and gentle boy, playing the piano, like his mother, and with a tendency towards religion. In the army, he was at first a chaplain's assistant. But he was sent to Europe as a soldier, survived the Battle of the Bulge, endured the hardship of running and hiding from the enemy behind enemy lines, was captured by the Germans, suffered a nervous breakdown as a prisoner and took mental flight from the reality of war. He witnessed the horrible firebombing of Dresden and its aftermath, cleared away rubble, and cremated human remains. After returning home, he entered optometry school and married the daughter of the owner of the school although he did not love her and was not attracted to her, but because he had withdrawn into himself after the shock of war, accepted whatever was as inevitable, and he did not find her disagreeable. He was, however, unable to adjust to civilian life and, in 1948, he signed himself into a mental hospital, presumably because of hallucinations: in his imagination he traveled to other time periods in his life. In the hospital, he met Eliot Rosewater, who introduced him to the science-fiction writing of Kilgore Trout. In his novels, Trout postulated life in a fourth dimension and criticized the brutality of life on earth. Influenced by Trout after reading some of his books, Billy began to imagine that he had been abducted by aliens whose philosophy of life was resignation to the inevitable and concentration on the beautiful moments of one's life. In addition, they believed that time had neither a beginning, middle, nor end, but that everything occurred simultaneously. With the psychic mechanism of escape into romantic daydreams based on the science-fiction stories he read to rely on, Billy led a rather normal and financially successful outer life, generous to his wife, powerless with his children, and secretly involved with an inner fantasy world which kept the trauma of the war years alive in him but also, by being transformed, out of reach. After suffering a head injury, however, in a plane crash, and after the death of his wife, he began to proselytize about his space travel and the philosophy he lived by, much to the displeasure of his neighbors and his children who thought him deranged. (103)

By making *Slaughterhouse-Five* a fragmented and discontinuous narrative told from Billy Pilgrim's point of view through the authoritative intermediary presence of a strong narrator, Vonnegut shaped the case history of an emotionally disturbed veteran with strange delusions into an ironic science-fiction tale. Casting a war story either as a psychological case history—look at the damage the terrible events of war cause to delicate humanity—or in the terms that Mary O'Hare deplores and that Roland Weary emulates, making it into a heroic John Wayne sort of macho romance, actually does not remove war from the common experience or make it terrible. Rather those sorts of presentations integrate it: they make war a part of human experience. War becomes exciting and an alternative fantasy adventure. But in *Slaughterhouse-Five*, war is deprived of its allure. Fascination is transposed away from war and attaches to a story about the effects of war on consciousness, the science-fiction fantasy adventure. In *Slaughterhouse-Five*, the final impression the reader is left with is not that the Tralfamadorian vision is absurd but that war is. Vonnegut leads readers into an experience of absurdity but prevents them from having the thrill of identification with the characters in the story that usually accompanies either the excitement of a romantic adventure or the torment of a case history. *Slaughterhouse-Five* is not interesting because of its plot or its characters but because of its bizarre construction, the off-kilter narrative presence, and its twilight-zone view of reality. Moreover, Vonnegut makes readers complicit with the narrator by making readers reconstruct the origins of Billy's malaise rather than presenting them in straightforward narrative.

Despite what Billy says, through the narrator, at the beginning of **chapter 2**, he has *not* come unstuck in time. Quite the opposite: he has become *stuck* in time. He is stuck in the moment before the bombing of Dresden, unable to live through the memory of the event, unable to remember it. Being stuck like that is what has immobilized him emotionally in his daily life and enabled him to escape from that daily life through his transformation into an interior voyager who can stoically negotiate a dimension of space and time usually inaccessible to mortals. The memory becomes unstuck towards the ends of **chapter 8**. A barbershop quartet begins to sing "That Old Gang of Mine" at an anniversary party for Billy and his wife, and as they do,

> Unexpectedly, Billy Pilgrim found himself upset by the song and the occasion. He had never had an old gang, old sweethearts and pals, but he missed one anyway, as the quartet made slow, agonized experiments with chords intentionally sour, sourer still, unbearably sour, and then a chord that was suffocatingly sweet, and then some sour ones again. Billy had powerful psychosomatic responses to the changing chords. His mouth filled with the taste of lemonade, and his face became grotesque, as though he

really were being stretched on the torture engine called the *rack*. (125)

Billy leaves the party, goes upstairs to his bedroom, and there, he "thought hard about the effect the quartet had had on him, and then found an association with an experience he had had a long time ago." Vonnegut makes the point, before he narrates it, of explaining that Billy "did not travel in time to the experience. He *remembered* it shimmeringly." (Emphasis added.) (129) Then, over several pages, Vonnegut describes the actual bombing of Dresden from Billy's point of view, how Billy was "down in the meat locker on the night Dresden was destroyed," how "there were sounds like giant footsteps above," how those "footsteps" were the sounds of "sticks of high-explosive bombs" blowing up. The guards went "to the head of the stairs every so often to see what it was like outside," and told on their return of "a firestorm out there." After the bombing was over, "[t]he guards drew together....they looked like a silent film of a barbershop quartet," which "might have been singing, 'So long forever, old sweethearts and pals.'" (130)

Once the bombing is over, Vonnegut continues the narrative for several pages only breaking the thread once to shift to a scene on Tralfamadore between Billy and Montana Wildhack, the movie siren who is his companion in the zoo there. She asks him to tell her a story, and he brings the memory of Dresden into the world of Tralfamadore and tells her the story of the bombing of Dresden and how "It was like the moon" afterwards. (130)

The attack of déjà vu is not the only disturbance of memory Billy suffers. He also does not remember reading Kilgore Trout's science-fiction novels until late in **chapter 9**, the penultimate chapter of *Slaughterhouse-Five*. Billy goes into an "adult" bookstore. But in the window and towards the front of the store, as a kind of decoy, rather than displaying the erotic merchandise, there is a collection of books by Kilgore Trout. While "everybody else in the store was pawing things," Billy picked up a Kilgore Trout novel and began to read. "He got a few paragraphs into it, and then realized that he *had* read it before—years ago, in the veterans' hospital." It is the prototype of his story. "It was about an Earthling man and woman who were kidnapped by extra-terrestrials" and "put on display on a planet called Zircon-212." (147) Vonnegut reveals both these fundamental and formative aspects of the plot late in the story and obliquely in the course of narrating other events, not directly. This technique gives credibility to an otherwise incredible plot. It seems to explain it and allows it to make sense inside the earth-defined world of the reader. By explaining it, however, Vonnegut risks explaining it away. But the impact of the book depends upon the viability of the Tralfamadore story. Despite, therefore, that finally the planet Tralfamadore is uncovered as quite likely a fantasy creation of a shell-shocked soldier—something like a compensatory sexual fantasy—because Vonnegut has presented the story as told by a strong, credible narrator from Billy's point of view, the Tralfamadore story is not so easy to explain away: it has taken hold of the reader's imagination, and in a sense has become real. By leading readers to believe, even temporarily, that the imaginary can be real, Vonnegut strengthens the possibility that readers can be helped to see that the real can be the result of a particular variety of imagination, the result of the ways we think and daydream. Mary O'Hare, the moral spirit of the book, has asserted in **chapter 1**: "she thought that wars were partly encouraged by books and movies." (11)

If the suppositions can be made to seem credible that reality depends upon imagination and that the reality we fashion creates the fantasies inside which we seek refuge from that reality, then it becomes reasonable to see the Tralfamadorian philosophy of resignation to inevitability that Billy advocates is not truth but a coping mechanism. Possibly, then, by imagining it differently, the world can be refashioned. Thus in *Slaughterhouse-Five*, Vonnegut offers the most appealing picture he can of an apathetic worldview and the most imaginative defense he can of resignation in order for readers not to accept apathy or resignation. He creates a world in which the birdsong that ends the book is all that can stand against horror.

It is a challenge to readers to do better and it is a strategy that accepts that it may be futile to write an anti-war novel, as he reports a film director tells him at the outset, (3) but necessary nevertheless.

Note

1. All references are to Vonnegut, Kurt. *Slaughterhouse Five*, Vintage, Random House: London, 1991

Critical Views

PETER J. REED ON THE STRUCTURE OF THE NOVEL

While *Slaughterhouse-Five* may appear to be wandering and random, an example of Vonnegut's tendencies toward the episodic and the digressive indulged to the extreme, it actually possesses an intricately designed structure. The author's description of his efforts to outline this story, climaxed by his making his "prettiest one" on the back of a roll of wallpaper with his daughter's crayons, seems entirely appropriate. Billy Pilgrim is at one point described as trying to reinvent or restructure his life, while in telling the story Vonnegut tries to give form to the same experiences. At the center of Vonnegut's material—in the wallpaper outline it is cross-hatched across the sheet—is the Dresden raid. From that central event he extends a web outward in time, space and characters. But "web" is a poor metaphor; one might as easily say that he "tunnels into" the experience to find its meaning. Time, space and event coexist and coalesce in this novel, and that is what the structure attempts to convey.

First Vonnegut sets up a frame for the story with the autobiographical prologue in the first chapter. An important preparation for this comes on the title page itself; between the title and a thumbnail biography of the author, Vonnegut describes his book as "A Duty Dance with Death." The autobiographical first chapter is matched by a return to more of the same in the last chapter, completing the frame, but in such a way as to integrate the frame with the main narrative. The framing device and the interrelationship of the autobiographical with the narrative are strengthened by periodic intrusions by the author throughout the novel: "I was there" or "that was me." "A Dance" is an apt description for the interwoven pattern of the narrative, with the author himself occasionally appearing as one of the dancers. All of the events portrayed are carefully interconnected, and events from "separate" times are often juxtaposed, completing or commenting upon one another. The frequent complementary nature of the time fragments adds to their coherence, although there is surprisingly little difficulty in following this seemingly disjointed narrative. The prologue to the first chapter, and the quick general guidelines to Billy's life in the second, provide the reader with a strong sense of direction from the outset.

The title page gives another clue to the structure of *Slaughterhouse-Five:* "This is a novel somewhat in the telegraphic schizophrenic manner of tales of the planet Tralfamadore, where the flying saucers come from." It might seem absurd to take such an obviously spoofing account at all seriously. The description of the Tralfamadorian novel represents characteristic Vonnegutian self-derision, like the portraits of Kilgore Trout, but as parody it makes some real sense. The Tralfamadorian novel is made up of "clumps of symbols" each of which "'is a brief, urgent message—describing a situation, a scene.'" Tralfamadorians read these simultaneously, not consecutively. "'There isn't any particular relationship between all the messages, except that the author has chosen them carefully, so that, when seen all at once, they produce an image of life that is beautiful and inspiring and deep.'" Aside from the fact that the Tralfamadorians, in their novels as in their minds, emphasize beautiful moments and exclude the unpleasant ones, *Slaughterhouse-Five* almost fits their requirements. Most of the situations described are grim, many downright painful. The "clumps of symbols" obviously cannot be read simultaneously, either, but the way in which short scenes from several points in time are spliced together does help sustain the impression of concurrent actions, and intensifies the sense of an interrelationship of events transcending time. Nor is there always a "particular relationship between all the messages," but they often do show a kinship of theme or image, and they cohere to create "an image of life" which, while not always "beautiful," is frequently "surprising" and in total effect quite "deep." Because all of its scenes cannot be read simultaneously, the book comes closer to possessing a climax than does the Tralfamadorian novel. It is hard to single out one climactic event, be it the raid itself or the ironic execution of Edgar Derby, but the novel certainly builds toward the end where the meaning, the questions and the emotional impact come together.

PETER J. REED ON THE CONTEXT OF DRESDEN

The moral and psychological context for the depiction of the Dresden raid is set up in the first chapter. There we see essentially two perspectives; the highly personal recollections of the author who was involved in the event, and the detached, distant view of history. The latter is introduced in the account of the destruction of Sodom and Gomorrah which the author reads in his motel Gideon Bible. It suggests that "Those were vile people in both those cities, as is well known. The world was better off without them." Obviously, he does not share that harsh moral view, and his sympathies lie with Lot's wife who looks back to where people and homes had been—an act he finds lovable because it is so human. The Biblical account provides a precedent for Dresden; a city destroyed in righteous wrath, people judged evil and ripe for annihilation, and an observer who looks back wonderingly, touched by human compassion. Some of the parallel moral questions posed by such great destructions are obvious. So the people of Sodom and Gomorrah were a bad lot—does that justify their obliteration? So the Germans had devastated Warsaw, Rotterdam, Coventry and East London, and had sent millions to their deaths in other ways—does that make moral the destruction of Dresden? Vonnegut makes considerable effort to incorporate official and historical assessments of such raids into his novel by quoting from President Truman's announcement of the atom-bombing of Hiroshima and from David Irving's book, *The Destruction of Dresden*. The Truman statement, made in time of war, essentially argues that the destruction of Hiroshima was necessary to save civilization from the destruction wreaked by the Japanese. The two forwards to Irving's book, written by Lieutenant General Ira C. Eaker, U.S.A.F., and Air Marshal Sir Robert Saundby, R.A.F., some time after the war, struggle with the moral issues, regretting so many deaths in a militarily unnecessary raid but insisting that they be viewed in the context of the even more massive slaughters wrought by the Germans.

Vonnegut's comment on these official assessments comes in the rambling words of Billy Pilgrim: "'If you're ever in Cody, Wyoming ... just ask for Wild Bob.'" Wild Bob was the colonel who had led his troops to disaster, lost his regiment, then tried to assure his soldiers they had "nothing to be ashamed of" because they had left a lot of Germans dead, too. Yet Wild Bob remains a sympathetic character. Perhaps through him Vonnegut observes that military men responsible for such slaughters act not out of malignity but from muddled values which prevent them from seeing simpler moral truths. Treated less sympathetically than the commander who makes a mistake is the military historian who later tries to justify the error. Illustrating this role is Bertram Copeland Rumfoord, "the official Air Force historian," writing his one volume history of the U.S.A.A.F. in World War II. He feels obliged to mention Dresden because so many people now know that it was worse than Hiroshima. The raid has been cloaked in secrecy for years lest it be criticized by "a lot of bleeding hearts," Rumfoord says, and he seems bent only on dismissing any notion that it might be a blemish on the glorious record of the Air Force. So intent is he on treating Dresden with official "detachment" that he shuts out any possible firsthand reports from Billy Pilgrim. He seems only concerned to convince Billy, as his readers, that "it *had* to be done"—while remaining rather uneasy himself.

Posed against the official assessments are episodes involving two lesser characters which serve to expose Dresden to a different moral viewpoint. The Sodom and Gomorrah reference, the allusion to Hiroshima and the historical judgments on Dresden all involve looking at the raid from a distance, taking an overview of it, placing it in a large historical context. The stories of Paul Lazarro and Edgar Derby, like those of Lot's wife and Billy Pilgrim, reverse the perspective, measuring the larger event against individual human consequences. Paul Lazarro typifies those miserable little men, inviting our pity as much as our disgust, who are as close as Vonnegut ever gets to creating villains. He threatens to have Billy killed, and actually does have him killed years later. In the prison camp he tries to steal an English officer's watch, gets caught in the act, and suffers a severe mauling. Characteristically, he swears he will have the Englishman killed—a stranger will knock at his door, announce he comes from Paul Lazarro, "shoot his pecker off," give him a couple of minutes to think about that, then kill him. He also tells a tender story of how he once fed a dog steak containing sharpened fragments of clocksprings. This twisted little crank feeds on revenge—"the sweetest thing in life"—yet he takes no satisfaction from the destruction of Dresden. He bears the Germans no grudge, and he prides himself on never harming an innocent bystander. The obvious moral object lesson here is that in some ways even a sordid monster like Lazarro can be superior to the saviors of civilization, who also take revenge, who kill those who have done them no harm in ways every bit as horrible as anything the warped mind of Lazarro could conceive and with no thought for innocent bystanders. The second incident involves Edgar Derby, who is arrested and shot by the Germans for plundering when caught with a perfectly ordinary teapot taken from a ruined house. This time we observe the irony of a society which condones massive destruction but which executes a man—one who tries bravely to be decent and moral—for salvaging a teapot from that wreckage.

These two minor incidents give scale to the inhumanity and moral dubiousness of the Dresden raid. The disaster itself remains so massive as to be hard to register in any other way. Statistics of the numbers killed and the houses destroyed, or descriptions of the ruins lying like the surface of the moon, remain too large, too general, too abstract. Particular images like human bodies reduced to charred logs or girls boiled alive in a water tower, and personal episodes like those involving Lazarro and Derby, stick in the mind. The same is true for Billy. The horror of the total nightmare registers in the little things, like the four distraught German guards, huddled together, mouths open but not knowing what to say, looking like a barbershop quartet singing (and here the irony borders on excess) "That Old Gang of Mine." "'So long forever,' old sweethearts and pals—God bless 'em—.'" And after all that he has suffered and the carnage he has witnessed among the debris, it takes the sight of those wretched horses drawing his cart to reduce Billy to tears.

The significance of the Dresden firestorm, then, is weighed on the scale of time, from Sodom and Gomorrah down to Hiroshima, and on the scale of human response, from the collective, public view of the official history to the personal nightmare of Billy Pilgrim. It is also measured spatially, in effect, through the perspective afforded by the use of science fiction. Billy tells the Tralfamadorians about wars on Earth, and what a great threat to all life the inhabitants of his planet must be. The Tralfamadorians regard his concerns as stupid. They know how the Universe ends, and Earth has nothing to do with it. Their own experiments with flying-saucer fuels end the Universe. In any case, they tell Billy, Tralfamadore is not as peaceful as he seems to think. They have wars as dreadful as anything Billy knows about. Once again the point of view of a more sophisticated being from another planet provides commentary on human behavior, yet this time it might surprise us as much as it does Billy. The Tralfamadorians' timeless view is not that Earthlings are senseless and barbaric to engage in war, a menace to themselves and the Universe. It is that Billy is ridiculous to expect such a logical projection of the future to work in an absurd Universe, and that he exaggerates the importance of the human role in the cosmos. In particular, he overemphasizes free will and fails to recognize that the tragedies of war and ultimate destruction occur, like all things, because that is the way the moment is structured. They advocate acceptance of life's cruelties and catastrophes, saying "so it goes" to each, then turning their thoughts to happier things.

That position has a certain undeniable logic, especially to beings capable of time-travel. For one thing, it avoids putting them constantly at odds with the essential nature of an Absurd Universe. For another, it makes sense given their conception of time, where past, present and future are all fixed and determinate. Whatever will be, is; whatever has been, is; whatever is, always has been and always will be. We need not accept the Tralfamadorian view of life to recognize that it represents a commentary on the human lot. For the events of the novel point to a world in which things happen which are beyond our control, in which what we try to control even with the best of intentions often goes awry, and where the forces which shape our destinies are beyond our comprehension even if they are more than simply "the structure of the moment." If the circumstances of existence are thus, then the motto which we are shown once hanging on Billy's wall and once hanging between Montana Wildhack's breasts—"God grant me the serenity to accept the things I cannot change, courage to change the things I can, and wisdom always to tell the difference"—proves ironic to say the least. As the narrator comments: "Among the things Billy Pilgrim could not change were the past, the present, and the future." Or, in other words, accept everything with serenity. Thus the lesson of Tralfamadore has much in common with the admonition to Lot's wife not to look back to Sodom and with Rumfoord's attitude of leaving the history of the Dresden raid as nearly forgotten as possible. It is also implicit in Vonnegut's saying that his book remains a failure because it was written by someone who, like Lot's wife, had been turned into a pillar of salt.

STANLEY SCHATT ON STREAM OF CONSCIOUSNESS IN THE NOVEL

Since Vonnegut has constructed *Slaughterhouse-Five* with the fire-bombing of Dresden at its center, all Billy's time travel and memories are linked to it by repression. Because Vonnegut apparently links the fire-bombing of Dresden with what to him is the very problem posed by Man's seemingly unbound proclivity for evil that he referred to in an earlier novel as the forces of "Mother Night," it is quite natural for him to show Billy trying to repress such a memory. Despite such efforts, Billy's repressed thoughts are part of his stream of consciousness though, even while in his sleep-like state, the actual holocaust is still to painful to face directly.

Vonnegut uses stream of consciousness, sensory impressions, and interior monologue to show that all of Billy's thoughts lead indirectly yet ultimately to Dresden and to the disturbing yet unanswerable question for him of why man destroys and kills. Billy begins one of his journeys through time as a German prisoner of war about to be given a shower in Dresden in 1944. When a German soldier turns on a master valve, the water is like "scalding rain." It "jangled Billy's skin without thawing the ice in the marrow of his long bones" (73). This sensation of being showered with hot water causes young Pilgrim to go back in time to his infancy. Suddenly he "was a baby who had just been bathed by his mother." In order to powder him, his mother takes him into "a rosy room ... filled with sunshine" (73). The remembrance of that sunshine upon him causes Billy to jump forward in time to a point when he is a "middle-aged optometrist again, playing hacker's golf ... on a blazing summer Sunday morning" (73). When he bends down to retrieve his golf ball safely trapped in the cup, Billy suddenly travels in time to the moment when he finds himself trapped by the Tralfamadorians, "strapped to a yellow contour chair ... aboard a flying saucer, which was bound for Tralfamadore" (73–74).

The logic behind this time shift appears to be his association with the word *trapped*. A Tralfamadorian tells him that all Tralfamadorians are like bugs trapped in amber, for "Only on Earth is there any talk of free will" (74). Billy has moved from taking a shower in Dresden in 1944 to talking to aliens on the planet Tralfamadore in 1967, but his focus is still on man's inhumanity exemplified by the Dresden holocaust; for, when he ponders the question of human free will, what he is really asking is, if man does indeed have free will, what rationale can he possibly have to explain his actions during the war, particularly his fire-bombing of Dresden.

While Vonnegut's use of a narrator with a personality all his own, his use of stream of consciousness, and his manipulation of the novel's time scheme and esthetic distance makes *Slaughterhouse-Five* a difficult book to follow, his strong feelings about the Dresden holocaust made such techniques necessary. Without such artistic slight-of-hand, the novel might have turned into a political diatribe or perhaps into a maudlin, introspective look at war.

Stanley Schatt on Vonnegut's View of War and Death

Slaughterhouse-Five is proof that Vonnegut kept his promise to write a war novel that does not glorify or glamorize killing. His novel does repudiate most of the stereotyped characters and patriotic bilge that has become standard movie fare. One of Billy's companions after the Battle of the Bulge is Roland Weary; he is stupid, fat, mean, and smells like bacon no matter how often he bathes; and he enjoys romanticizing the war until his daydreams blot out the reality of the frozen German landscape. While he is in reality unpopular, he imagines himself to be one of the three close war comrades who call themselves the "Three Musketeers." Vonnegut describes how Weary confronted Billy Pilgrim and "dilated upon the piety and heroism of 'The Three Musketeers,' portrayed, in the most glowing and impassioned hues, their virtue and magnanimity, the imperishable honor they acquired for themselves, and the great services they rendered to Christianity" (44).

Weary's fantasy is counterpointed by Vonnegut's earlier description about an early Christian crusade—by the shocking reality of a children's crusade in which young boys are butchered or sold into slavery because of a war they cannot even comprehend. Vonnegut further deflates the idea that war is glorious and fun by describing a group of English prisoners of war who live in a self-supervised camp that they keep immaculate and well stocked with goods. They exercise regularly, keep themselves well bathed and groomed, and manage to preserve an atmosphere of normalcy. It is not surprising that the German commander adores them because "they were exactly what Englishmen ought to be. They made war look stylish and reasonable, and fun" (81). The British prisoners are unaware that the soap and candles they use were made from "the fat of rendered Jews and gypsies and fairies and communists, and other enemies of the state" (83). It is more than coincidental that they entertain Billy Pilgrim's group of bedraggled American prisoners by performing an adult version of Cinderella. They reinforce the German commander's justification for the war by transforming the ugly, horrifying realities of war into something beautiful and magical. But midnight tolls, and Billy once again sees the real picture of warfare when he goes outside to move his bowels. He finds all his fellow Americans terribly sick with diarrhea and suddenly becomes snagged to a barbwire fence.

Vonnegut suggests that the United States Air Force tried to transform the Dresden fire-bombing from an atrocity to something almost heroic. While in a hospital recovering from an accident, Billy Pilgrim meets Bertram Copeland Rumfoord, a retired brigadier general in the Air Force Reserve and the official Air Force Historian. Rumfoord examines David Irving's *The Destruction of Dresden* because he is interested in the forewords by retired Lieutenant General Ira C. Eaker and by British Air Marshall Sir Robert Saundby. Eaker concludes his foreword by pointing out that, while he regrets that 135,000 people were killed in the fire-bombing of Dresden, he feels far worse about the five million Allies killed in the effort to destroy Nazism. As Donald J. Greiner has noted, Vonnegut despises Eaker's reasoning since the general apparently believed that the balancing of one atrocity with another by the other side neutralizes both and expiates all guilt.[11]

Saundby's foreword, on the other hand, points out that the Dresden attack was not a military necessity; it was merely an unfortunate incident caused by circumstances. The men who approved the attack were not evil or cruel, but they may have been too remote from the reality of the war to understand the destruction such an attack would bring. Such a point of view is much closer to Vonnegut's reaction to the atrocity. Rumfoord reveals that the Dresden bombing has not heretofore been a part of the official Air Force history of World War II "for fear that a lot of bleeding hearts ... might not think it was such a wonderful thing to do" (165). Vonnegut finds such reasoning reprehensible.

While *Slaughterhouse-Five* is about the Dresden air attack and about World War II, its major focus is on death. Many deaths in the novel are ironic, especially that of unfortunate school teacher Edgar Derby who survives the Battle of the Bulge only to be shot for plundering a teapot from the ruins of the smoldering city. Vonnegut offers another view of death when he describes the Tralfamadorian view that all moments always have and always will exist and that death is just one moment in anyone's life. The Tralfamadorians enjoy the good moments and ignore the bad moments, but this solution is unsatisfactory to Vonnegut who believes that death is far too important to ignore.

Vonnegut's view of death becomes clear in the final chapter of *Slaughterhouse-Five* in which he describes not his visit to Dresden in 1968 but Billy Pilgrim's efforts to dig up the bodies buried beneath the rubble of the fire-bombed city. When Billy is released from captivity, Vonnegut describes the scene as follows:

> And somewhere in there was springtime. The corpse mines were closed down. The soldiers all left to fight the Russians.... And then one morning, they got up to discover that the door was unlocked. World War Two in Europe was over.
> Billy and the rest wandered out onto the shady street. The trees were leafing out. There was nothing going on out there, no traffic of any kind. There was only one vehicle, an abandoned wagon drawn by two horses. The wagon was green and coffin shaped.
> Birds were talking.
> One bird said to Billy Pilgrim, "Poo-tee-weet?" (186).

Billy's world is filled with both life and death. Though it is spring and the trees are leafing out, the coffin-shape of the abandoned wagon serves as a reminder of death surrounding him. The last word in the novel is the bird's message to Billy Pilgrim, and it is the same message Eliot Rosewater received as *God Bless You, Mr. Rosewater* concluded. As Raymond Olderman has pointed out in *Beyond the Wasteland*, "Poo-tee-weet represents a 'cosmic cool,' a way of viewing life with the distance necessary to cope with the horrors that both Billy Pilgrim and Eliot Rosewater experience."[12] It is not callousness or indifference but merely a defense mechanism that allows Vonnegut to smile through his tears and to continue to live and to write.

Slaughterhouse-Five concludes with Vonnegut himself describing among othe things the latest casualty lists in Vietnam, the death of his father, the assassination of Robert Kennedy, the execution of Kindly Edgar Derby, and the end of World War II. Though Vonnegut sees the Dresden fire-bombing in the context of the political assassinations and of the unpopular war that overshadowed almost all other issues in the 1960's, he is able to smile through his tears and provide an affirmation of life. The message of *Slaughterhouse-Five* is the need for compassion; Malachi Constant (*The Sirens of Titan*) and Billy Pilgrim both learn that the purpose of life, no matter whether there is free will or not, is to love whomever is around to be loved.

Notes

11. David J. Greiner, "Vonnegut's *Slaughterhouse-Five* and the fiction of Atrocity," *Critique*, XIV (1973), 43.

12. Raymond Olderman, *Beyond the Wasteland: A Study of the American Novel in the Nineteen-Sixties* (New Haven: Yale University Press, 1972), p. 211.

RICHARD GIANNONE ON THE NOVEL AS MORAL TESTIMONY

Slaughterhouse-Five opens with numerous snagged beginnings that produce a humility rite for Vonnegut through a confession of inadequacy. The fire-bombing of Dresden, which was an open city without defense or military importance, proves inexplicable to him. A recent visit to the city deepens his anxiety, for he finds that modern technology has remade a Baroque art center into a Dayton, Ohio. He tries to outline the Dresden story but comes up with child's play. Calamity becomes decoration; orange cross-hatchings on a roll of wallpaper insult the 135,000 lives consumed in the holocaust. Tourist guides and histories are nostalgic forms to a city that is no more. Vonnegut then turns inward to ponder the moral geography limned by the devastated physical one. Roehke and Cèline are promptings toward honesty, but only that. As a last resort he goes to Genesis, the story of first things, to learn from other holocausts in other times. But the raining of fire and brimstone on Sodom and Gomorrah in the Old Testament seems a just act compared to the airplane assaults on Dresden simply for being there, vulnerable and beautiful.

No wonder the first words of the novel proclaim fallibility. "All this happened, more or less." The opening words introduce an unstable verisimilitude where merge true and false, past and future, here and there, inner space and outer space. This coalescing on many levels carries with it a repudiation of facts that makes our reading an ironic exercise. We learn to distrust history. Historical judgment is founded in causality, which this novel negates. The last word of history is the first word of *Slaughterhouse-Five*. We see the wiping out of "The Florence on the Elbe" as so gratuitous, so nihilistic that to call it victory, as history does, debases language. The facts of the bombing are pointedly confused in the novel. Actually a British plan, in the novel it seems an American scheme. The effect of blurring facts shifts the emphasis from political settlement to moral outcome. In moral terms, we are all responsible for the slaughter. And as we follow the narrator-witness through postwar American life, we lose any sense that the county won World War II.

Vonnegut's testimony puts a moral light on war to reveal alliances not shown by treaties. The essential battle here is waged by man against the violent bent in himself. Vonnegut plumbs the dark forces in the human spirit. Sentimentality, egoism, blind patriotism, materialism, these are the enemy; and for Vonnegut they are the signal qualities of American life. Against them stand conscience and feeling. Vonnegut, the witness, acts as a moral scout, smuggling himself across battle lines to reach the front of consciousness where he hopes to find final resistance to killing. His moral awareness accounts for the uncommon affection for a cherished city of the declared enemy and for the German people themselves. They are presented as fellow human beings struggling against their own propensity for violence. And to the degree that Americans yielded to their destructive urge (the violent style of postwar American life suggests a *high* degree), they—we—fell victims. Bother political sides lost in the struggle for human decency.

As the Gospels use the Old Testament, so the novel uses an Old Testament figure to characterize the moral stance of the witness to Dresden. "I've finished my war book now," Vonnegut says at the end of the first chapter. The next one I write is going to be fun. This one is a failure, and had to be, since it was written by a pillar of salt." The model of survival is Lot's wide, who, the novel explains, was turned into a pillar of salt for looking back on the smoldering ruins of Sodom and Gomorrah, which she had escaped. Though sparred by God's mercy, she suffered from the warmth of her own mercy. Vonnegut, the witness to Dresden, whose survival from disaster is also his fate, draws strength from seeing how a gesture of helpless love redefines its fatal expression. Once again, the reader sees that failure can be positive in effect on others. Where triumph is born of slaughter, defeat can hold dignity by preserving our capacity to care for others. The Old Testament allusion locates the novel's tonal center at the edge of devastation in a state of grief. The evocation of Lot's wife is technically apt, too. She endured a great deal but knew little, so the pillar of salt protects the novel from settling into the inaccuracies of rationality or conclusiveness.

The narrator-witness evangelizes for love by telling the life not of a savior of the world but of a hapless wanderer through the universe. Billy Pilgrim is a man of our time who floats through events, taking the shape they give him. He is a middle-American. He was born in 1922, the year of Vonnegut's birth, son of a barber in the direful city of Ilium, New York, serves in World War II, then prospers as an optometrist in a suburban shopping center, drives an El Dorado Coupe deVille with bumper stickers encouraging people to support our local police and to visit the Ausable Chasm and, between those devotions, to impeach Earl Warren. The scenario for The Good Life has a part for him. Billy owns his piece of the action in which the American bourgeois success drama is now played—"a fifth of the new Holiday Inn out on Route 54, and half of three Tastee-Freeze stands." And Billy is a family man. Married to Valencia Merble, he has fathered one daughter, Barbara, and one son, Robert, a decorated Green Beret who got "all straightened out" in Vietnam from his exuberant pastimes, such as tipping over tombstones. The Pilgrims' home once even had a dog named Spot running around it. The underside of Billy's life follows the other formula of our time: mental breakdown, shock therapy, emptiness.

Billy's life is so stereotypical that an account of it inevitably takes on a contemptuous tone that conceals his specialness. For one thing, he, like Eliot Rosewater, is gentle despite pressure to be competitive and cruel. During the war he is a friendless servant to servicemen—"a valet to a preacher, expected no promotions or medals, bore no arms, and had a meek faith in a loving Jesus which most soldiers found putrid." Many survived the war; Billy survived with his tender concern for other intact. For him knowledge is for sharing, not controlling others. One night in 1967 he is mysteriously kidnapped by a flying saucer to the planet Tralfamadore. He asks his green hosts on Tralfamadore: "So tell me the secret so I can take it back to earth and save us all: How can a planet live at peace?" The message from outer space and his commitment to preach it are other marks of Billy's distinctiveness.

The Tralfamadorians do not answer the question verbally, but they do respond by closing "their little hands on their eyes." They demonstrate how to live at peace: concentrate on the happy moments of life and ignore the unhappy ones or "stare only at pretty things as eternity failed to go by." The Tralfamadorian technique of managing pain recalls the way a child may exercise some control over the environment through vision. Shutting the eyes creates the blank which serves to wipe out undesired incidents. The habit may liberate the person from pain; but it may also isolate, because the disappearance of unwelcome sights sets the beholder apart from the universe that is banished. Separated from the actuality it transforms, fantasy can be destructively overwhelming to the dreaming mind. We will see in *Slaughterhouse-Five*, as we saw in the engulfing pretense in *Mother Night*, that self-blinding may create a swift regression to a death-like unconsciousness. Great psychic risk, then, accompanies the inner peace that Billy learns how to develop on Tralfamadore.

The benefit of the new tranquility is not only a release from danger but also a privileged glimpse into time. Disparate moments from the past and from the future can be projected onto the blank made by the covering of eyes. Billy makes many trips through the fourth dimension; each of them permits him to see as whole and coherent his otherwise fragmented life. He can go to sleep a widower and wake up on his wedding day; he walks through a door in 1955, goes out another in 1941, and goes back through the same door in 1963. "'The Tralfamadorians can look at all the different moments just the same way we can look at a stretch of the Rocky Mountains....'"

Billy's pleasant experience on Tralfamadore is complemented by Kilgore Trout's *The Gospel from Outer Space*, given to him by Eliot Rosewater, a fellow veteran suffering a similar mental collapse. Trout's book concerns a visitor "shaped very much like a Tralfamadorian" who on coming to Earth sees a flaw in the New Testament's emphasis on the divinity of Jesus at the expense of the rest of humanity and goes on to revise the historical Gospels to suit the present needs of the suffering nobodies of the world by teaching their potential divine adoption. No longer can lynchers nail a nobody to a cross and get away with it:

…just before the nobody dies, the heavens opened up,
and there was thunder and lightning. The voice of God

came crashing down. He told the people that he was adopting the bum as his son, giving him the full powers and privileges of The Son of the Creator of the Universe throughout all eternity. God said this: *From this moment on, He will punish horribly anybody who torments a bum who has no connections!*

The new Gospel makes the world safe for the spiritually disenfranchised. Its saving message is the consolation that the fragments made from living on Earth recommend a person to God. Trout's theology from outer space enables Billy Pilgrim to comprehend himself as one who is set apart from other persons to be included in the drama of salvation. The new Gospel makes life possible for him because it does not deny his paltriness.

Slaughterhouse-Five leaves no doubt that the science-fiction world of Tralfamadore helps Billy. But in a work whose skepticism toward science and technology runs deep and whose style makes the largest possible claim for ambivalence, we would do well to consider the teachings of Trout's *The Gospel from Outer Space* more fully than its fantasy truths would invite. The validity of Trout's Gospel derives from the structure of the world producing it. Outer space lies outside of time. We can evaluate the new Gospel and the Tralfamadorian message by observing the effects on Billy of taking time a function of seeing. When his experiences are lined up like so many mountains before his eyes, good and bad moments stand without individual emphasis. Mental disposition is a matter of picking and choosing. So happiness, the desired state, arises not from inner fulfillment but from external visual selection, focusing on "pretty things as eternity failed to go by." By ignoring moments that threaten to crash in on him, such as war, Billy gains control over them. The disquieting experience is there but he is spared its devastating effect. This negating way of handling pain alters Billy's deepest experience of his own being. He can abdicate any need to explain the world around him because moments locked in their discreteness present a world without causality. Fear disappears because fear is causality internalized, molded by an expectation of danger. Where effects do not connect with causes, ambition, anxiety, and anger cannot be felt. Without a measurement between effects there is no change. Finally, the mind masters death, the ultimate change. Billy is forever ready for the shot from a high-powered laser gun that kills him. He reports his several encounters with his murder in calm tones on a tape recorder: *"I, Billy Pilgrim...will die, have died, and always will die on February thirteenth, 1976."* The veteran of Dresden dies precisely on the thirty-first anniversary of the fire-bombing.

Billy's death moment is further revealing. The backhand salute to the nation's bicentennial measures the completeness with which Billy's painful middle-class story is a product of American political history, which has been a chronicle of aggressive pursuit of money and violence. The circumstances of his murder epitomize the violence at large in America. Billy is preaching to a large crowd of prospective converts in Chicago on his favorite Tralfamadorian subjects of time and flying saucers, and we can recognize the riotous 1968 Chicago Democratic Convention turned into a revival meeting with the side act of assassination that frequently punctuates our history. The reader is not surprised that Earth should make and unmake Billy so barbarously. We see, too, that his new technique of blinking away unpleasant moments fails to moderate the pain of the event. The horror show is made more horrible by Billy's supercool rendering of his annihilation. Tralfamadorian detachment consoles by denying death, but the absence of Billy's terror is itself a terror. Only by removing emotion can he deal with the world.

The self created by science fiction lacks the tension that makes people human. Billy's estrangement from the world and from himself requires new ways of understanding because the events are too bizarre for his old notions of free will and responsibility; but Tralfamadorian wisdom does not go beyond negation. It acknowledges absurdity and it does less immediate damage to his mind than do the convulsions of electroshock therapy he undergoes at the hospital and the subsequent shock-treatment of bourgeois comfort, but it leaves him insentient.

The new Gospel, then, is an equivocal document. It is what it comes from: all is space, so it addresses the spatialized, one-dimensional person. The so-called happy moments are based on lack of emotion. The genial manner of Billy's green friends disguises the violence submerged in their apathy. They, and not earthlings playing with bombs, bring an end to the universe. (Another blow to the human ego.)

> "How—how *does* the universe end?" said Billy.
> "we blow it up, experimenting with new fuels for our flying saucers. A Tralfamadorian test pilot presses a starter button, and the whole Universe disappears." So it goes.

Their apocalyptic calm is born of total indifference. Since they do not change, they have no ethical reference. The opposite of Lot's wife, they know a great deal but care not at all. They play God by without his merciful concern for creation. The Tralfamadorian self embodies the scientific ideal and thereby exposes its shortcoming. The fiction about science is that it acts in a moral vacuum; the truth is that when doing so, science creates that vacuum. These truths we know from *Cat's Cradle*. Tralfamadore is a grim world of mechanical wizardry and moral impoverishment, a World's Fair writ large without anyone around sensible enough to question its appalling impassiveness. We can see why Billy is drawn to the new Gospel: it reinvents his person according to the functional specifications of technology. At the same time, we are alerted that Billy's desire to free himself from the destructive forces of actual earthy life ends with a Tralfamadorian unfeeling reduction to it.

Billy's need to remake himself is never questioned; the manner in which he does so is. Both Billy and Eliot Rosewater "were dealing with similar crises in similar ways. They had both found life meaningless, partly because of what they had seen in the war....So they were trying to re-invent themselves and their universe." The ascendency of science fiction implies a failure of Christianity, which serves as model for Trout's new

Gospel. Men are caught between two testaments. One is from a remote ancient world; the other from a far-out contemporary world. Both testaments are crucial, for they shape Billy's person. The novel invites us to consider their claims and the foundations of selfhood they lay.

The New Testament reckons time from Jesus' birth. Time is a motion backward and forward. The backward flow is preparation for Jesus: the forward thrust from his birth, as our calendars indicated, is toward the End. The self of Christianity is, then, precisely time. "This is the seriousness of time and timing," Tillich says. "Through our timing God times the coming of His kingdom; through our timing He elevates the time of vanity into the time of fulfillment."[1] As there are two times, there are two selves, the vain one of this world which is transformed into a self of the eschaton beyond time. Vonnegut implies that the Christian Gospel sense of time seems inadequate to transform our lives. On the other hand, the End has not yet happened, though it was pronounced imminent nearly 2000 years ago, so we take the apocalyptic imagination and its redemptive hope less seriously. On the other hand, having witnessed of late The War To End All Wars, The Third Reich, Dresden (135,000 dead), Tokyo (83,793(, Hiroshima (71,379(, Vietnam (to be calculated), we have adopted a post-apocalyptic callousness about the modern situation. What End can rival what we have already witnessed?[2]

The Gospel from Outer Space does speak to our sense of crisis by proposing an eschatology of the single moment. Our sense of collapse is ratified by its nominalism. Its appeal, however, expresses its limitation. "If what Billy Pilgrim learned from the Tralfamadorians is true," Vonnegut says, "that we will all live forever, not matter how dead we may sometimes seem to be, I am not overjoyed." A self without death is a self without transcendence. Trout's new Gospel gives destruction history where the Christian Gospels offer salvation history.

There is, in sum, a tension among three shaping forces in *Slaughterhouse-Five*: the ancient Christian news of victory over death; the Tralfamadorian message of no death; and the message implied in the reader's unfolding consciousness about the respective choices of each message. This deepening consciousness is Vonnegut's gospel. I would put their respective views of self in this way: whereas the Christian self exists between vanity and fulfillment, the science-fiction self is eternally in isolation. Vonnegut, working against both views, seeks to measure the self's relatedness in mutuality through its capacity to grow in consciousness and compassion. Vonnegut's new covenant stipulates the obligation of spiritual nurturance among persons.

Notes

1. Pall Tillich, *The New Being* (New York: Charles Scribner's Sons, 1955), p. 103.

2 See Frank Kermode, *The Sense of an Ending: Studies in the Theory of Fiction* (New York: Oxford University Press, 1967).

JAMES LUNDQUIST ON THE "NEW REALITY" OF SLAUGHTERHOUSE-FIVE

"I felt after I finished *Slaughterhouse-Five* that I didn't have to write at all anymore if I didn't want to," Vonnegut has said. "It was the end of some sort of career."[4] *Slaughterhouse-Five*, with its non-linear time scheme and its complex interweaving of science-fiction fantasy and the realities of World War II, makes his earlier novels, as innovative as some of them are, appear to be ordinary and uncomplicated by comparison, even if they are far from being that. The reason for this is that Vonnegut reveals himself in *Slaughterhouse-Five*, as do Alexander Trocchi in *Cain's Book* and Thomas Pynchon in *V*, to be "highly self-conscious of the novel as an abstract concept that examines a condition that never yields itself up completely as itself."[5] In other words, the novel functions to reveal new viewpoints in somewhat the same way that the theory of relativity broke through the concepts of absolute space and time. *Slaughterhouse-Five* thus gains its structure from Vonnegut's essential aesthetic problem—how to describe a reality that is beyond human imagination.

The method he chooses is outlined in the explanation given Billy Pilgrim of the Tralfamadorian novel as he is being transported toward that whimsical planet. His captors offer him the only book in English they have, Jacqueline Susann's *Valley of the Dolls*, which is to be placed in a museum. "Billy read it, thought it was pretty good in spots," Vonnegut writes. "The people in it certainly had their ups and downs. But Billy didn't want to read about the same ups and downs over and over again."

The Tralfamadorians allow him to look at some of their novels, but warn that he cannot begin to understand them. The books are small; it would take a dozen of them to even approach *Valley of the Dolls* in bulk, and the language is impossible for Billy. But he can see that the novels consist of clumps of symbols with stars in between. Billy is told that the clumps function something like telegrams, with each clump a message about a situation or scene. But the clumps are not read sequentially as the chapters are in an earthling novel of the ordinary sort. They are read simultaneously. "There isn't any particular relationship between all the messages," the speaker says to Billy, "except that the author has chosen them carefully, so that, when seen all at once, they produce an image of life that is beautiful and surprising and deep. There is no beginning, no middle, no end, no suspense, no moral, no causes, no effects. What we love in our books are the depths of many marvelous moments seen all at one time."

Slaughterhouse-Five is an approximation of this type of novel. Its chapters are divided into short sections (clumps if you will), seldom more than a few paragraphs long. The time-tripping, both by Billy and the narrator, produces an effect somewhat like that achieved in the Tralfamadorian novel—to see many moments at once. The time-tripping also serves to eliminate suspense. (We know not only of Billy's assassination long before the novel ends, but also how the universe will end—the Tralfamadorians blow it up experimenting with a new fuel for their flying saucers.) And the conclusion Vonnegut comes to after examining the causes and effects of Dresden is that there indeed is no moral, only the *Poo-tee-weet* of the bird call that

Billy hears when he discovers that the war in Europe is over and he wanders out onto the shady streets of springtime Dresden.

What the Tralfamadorian structure does for Vonnegut is to enable him to embody a new reality in his novel—at least new in contrast to the sequential ups-and-downs reality of the traditional novel. Vonnegut's method accords well with the major changes in the conception of physical reality that have come out of contemporary science. "Change, ambiguity, and subjectivity (in a sense these are synonyms) thus become ways of defining human reality," Jerry H. Bryant writes in commenting on the relationship between twentieth-century physics and recent fiction. "Novelist after novelist examines these features, and expresses almost universal frustration at being deprived of the old stability of metaphysical reality."[6] But not Vonnegut. His Tralfamadorian scheme enables him to overcome the problems of change, ambiguity, and subjectivity involved in objectifying the events surrounding the fire-bombing of Dresden and the involvement of Billy Pilgrim and the author in them.

This is a difficult idea, but one way to understand it is to consider the distinction Bertrand Russell makes in *The ABC of Relativity* between the old view of matter (that it has a definite identity in space and time) and the new view (that it is an event). "An event does not persist and move, like the traditional piece of matter," Russell writes; "it merely exists for a little moment then ceases. A piece of matter will thus be resolved into a series of events.... The whole series of these events makes up the whole history of the particle, and the particle is regarded as *being* its history, not some metaphysical entity to which things happen."[7]

This is just the paradoxical conception of Billy that Vonnegut develops. Billy at first seems to be merely an entity to which things happen—he is lost behind the lines during the Battle of the Bulge, he and Roland Weary are captured by the Germans, he survives the fire-bombing of Dresden, he marries, he is the sole survivor of a plane crash, he hallucinates that he is kidnapped by the Tralfamadorians, he appears on crackpot talk-shows, and he is finally gunned down in Chicago. But through the constant movement back and forth in time that constitutes Vonnegut's narrative, we see Billy becoming his history, existing all at once, as if he is an electron. And this gives the novel a structure that is, to directly state the analogy, atomic. Billy whirls around the central fact of Dresden, the planes of his orbits constantly intersecting, and where he has been, he will be.

Of course, all of Vonnegut's earlier central characters are somewhat like Billy in that they are seen as aspects of a protean reality. (Again, the name of Paul Proteus suggests how persistent this representation of personality is.) But it is not until *Slaughterhouse-Five* that Vonnegut develops a way of fully representing the context of that reality. The sudden changes that come over Malachi Constant, Eliot Rosewater, and others make them seem as illusive and problematic as the absurd universe they occupy. By oversimplifying his characters, Vonnegut does manage to suggest something of the complexity of human nature by indirection. But they still tend to linger in the mind as cartoon figures (the Dell paperback covers of *The Sirens of Titan* and *Mother Night* certainly suggest so).

This is not the case with Billy Pilgrim. The Tralfamadorian structure through which his story is told (*sent* might be a better word) gives Billy dimension and substance and brings him eerily to life despite his pale ineffectuality. "Vonnegut's reluctance to depict well-developed characters and to supply them with conventional motives for their actions serves as a conscious burlesque of the whole concept of realism in the novel," Charles B. Harris in his study of the contemporary novel of the absurd has pointed out.[8] But with *Slaughterhouse-Five*, the conscious burlesque is diminished because Vonnegut has come up with a representation of Billy Pilgrim's universe that is in itself a new concept of realism—or reality.

Slaughterhouse-Five is thus as much a novel about writing novels as it is an account of Billy Pilgrim and Dresden. In relating the difficulty he had in dealing with Dresden, Vonnegut prefaces *Slaughterhouse-Five* with an account of his own pilgrimages through time as he tried to write about his

Dresden experience. The opening section consists of jumps back and forth in the author's life—from his return to Dresden on a Guggenheim grant to his return home from the war two decades earlier, from a conversation on the telephone with his old war buddy to the end of the war in a beet field on the Elbe outside of Halle, and then on to the Chicago City News Bureau, Schenectady and General Electric, visiting O'Hare in Pennsylvania, teaching writing at the University of Iowa, and then Dresden and the Guggenheim trip once more.

The concern is always with the problem of writing the book—how to represent imaginatively things that are unimaginable—but in detailing his frustrations, Vonnegut conceptualizes his own life the way he later does Billy's, in terms of Tralfamadorian time theory. The structure of the chapter about writing the novel consequently prefigures the structure of the novel itself.

In that opening section, Vonnegut outlines his essential difficulty by elaborating on the misconception with which he began work on the novel. He states that he thought the book would be easy to write—all he would have to do is to simply report what he had seen. But this does not work. Too many other things get in the way. Why was Dresden, a supposedly safe city, bombed? Why did the American and British governments cover up the facts about the raid? What does the Dresden attack imply about American and British civilization? And, more important, why must Vonnegut's life always lead up to and go back to what he saw when he emerged from the slaughterhouse meat locker and looked at the moonscape that was once perhaps the most beautiful city in Europe?

The conflict Vonnegut is indicating is that of the old Henry James-H. G. Wells debate on what the novel as a literary form should be. James felt that it should be mimetic, realistic, that it should relate human experience as accurately as possible through detailed characterization and careful construction. Wells, on the other hand, believed that social pronouncements and ideas are more important, and that art should be subordinate to both. Wells was not even certain that the novel should be taken seriously as an art form. For him, characterization was just something to be got through so that an idea or a "ventilation" of the novel's social, political, or philosophical point can be got across as clearly as possible.[9]

Wells's influence is certainly a factor in the development of the science-fiction novel, and James must be taken into account in any discussion of the so-called mainstream or art novel. Vonnegut, as he indicates in his preface to *Slaughterhouse-Five*, is caught somewhere in the middle of the debate. His earlier books are mainly novels of character written to a thesis, an approach that leads to the direct statement of a moral in *Mother Night*.

But *Slaughterhouse-Five* is different; Vonnegut's impulse is to begin with his own experience, not with characters or ideas, but the ideas soon get in the way.

Two structural possibilities come to mind. The first is suggested in the song Vonnegut remembers as he thinks about how useless, yet how obsessive, the Dresden part of his memory has been:

My name is Yon Yonson,
I work in Wisconsin,
I work in a lumbermill there,
The people I meet when I walk down the street,
They say, "What's your name?"
And I say,
"My name is Yon Yonson,
I work in Wisconsin...."

When people ask him what *he* is working on, Vonnegut says that for years he has been telling them the same thing—a book about Dresden. Like Yon Yonson, he seems doomed to repeat the answer endlessly. But the maddening song suggests something else—the tendency many people (perhaps all) have to return to a central point in their lives in reply to the question of identity ("What's your name?").

The song also crudely suggests the time theory that is later developed in the novel with its emphasis on infinite repetition. But repetition leads nowhere, especially in a novel, so

Vonnegut considers another possibility. He takes a roll of wallpaper, and on the back of it tries to make an outline of the story using his daughter's crayons (a different color for each of the characters). "And the blue line met the red line and then the yellow line," Vonnegut writes, "and the yellow line stopped because the character represented by the yellow line was dead. And so on. The destruction of Dresden was represented by a vertical band of orange cross-hatching, and all the lines that were still alive passed through it, came out the other side." This is an outline for a Jamesian novel with an essentially linear time scheme. But it does not work as a representation of the experience Vonnegut is anxious to write about.

For one thing, characters do not actually come out the other side and inevitably go on from there. Like Vonnegut himself, like Yon Yonson, they compulsively return, moving back and forth on their lines. And as for the lines that stop, the beginning and middle of those lines are still there. What does Vonnegut do? He comes up with a structure that includes both the Yon Yonson story and the wallpaper outline. It is as if he rolls the wallpaper into a tube so all of the characters and incidents are closely layered, so they are in effect one unit, and the reader must look at them from the side. The tube then becomes a telescope through which the reader looks into the fourth dimension, or at least into another dimension of the novel. The story goes around and around, yet it still leads somewhere, and yet the end is very close to the beginning.

It may well be that, as Karen and Charles Wood suggest, *Slaughterhouse-Five* is a new form of novel repesenting the mature fusion of science fiction and Jamesian literature of experience.[10]

Notes

4. Kurt Vonnegut Jr., *Wampeters, Foma & Granfalloons* (New York: Delta, 1975), p. 280.

5. Jerry H. Bryant. *The Open Decision* (New York: Free Press, 1970), p. 36.

6. Bryant, p. 22.

7. Bertrand Russell, *The ABC of Relativity* (London: Kegan Paul, 1925), p. 209.

8. Charles B. Harris, *Contemporary American Novelists of the Absurd* (New Haven: College and University Press, 1971), p. 74.

9. For a detailed study of the Wells-James debate, see Leon Edel and Gordon N. Ray, *Henry James and H.G. Wells* (Urbana: University of Illinois Press, 1958).

10. Karen and Charles Wood, "The Vonnegut Effect: Science Fiction and Beyond," in *The Vonnegut Statement*, p. 154.

WILLIAM RODNEY ALLEN ON THE USE OF TIME IN THE NOVEL

Put most simply, what Vonnegut says about time in the novel is that it does not necessarily "point" only in one direction, from past to future. As Lundquist observes, "The novel functions to reveal new viewpoints in somewhat the same way that the theory of relativity broke through the concepts of absolute space and time."[8] Twenty years after the publication of *Slaughterhouse-Five*, theoretical physicists like Stephen F. Hawking are becoming more convinced that there is no reason why under some circumstances the "arrow of time" might point from future to past rather than from past to future.[9] If such a reversal is possible, then the famous description in *Slaughterhouse-Five* of a backwards movie (in which air force planes suck up bombs into themselves from the ground and fly backwards to their bases, where soldiers unload the bombs and ship them back to the factories to be disassembled) might be more than a wistful fantasy of a peaceful world. Of course, Vonnegut is less interested in new theories in physics than he is in his characters' confrontations with a world that makes no sense in terms of their old ways of seeing it. Hence, rather than beginning his story by quoting Einstein, Vonnegut puts a particular person in a very particular situation: "Listen: Billy Pilgrim has come unstuck in time."

But that striking opening sentence comes not in chapter 1 but in chapter 2. Chapter 1 consists of Vonnegut speaking in his own voice about the difficulties of writing *Slaughterhouse-Five*. Beginning with his 1966 introduction to the reissued *Mother Night*, Vonnegut had begun to speak more openly about himself and about the autobiographical connections underlying his writing. In the opening and closing chapters of *Slaughterhouse-Five*, however, he takes that process much further. By making the autobiographical "frame" of the novel part of the novel itself (rather than setting those sections apart as a preface and an afterword) Vonnegut, as Lundquist puts it, "conceptualizes his own life the way he later does Billy's, in terms of Tralfamadorian time theory. The structure of the chapter about writing the novel consequently prefigures the structure of the novel itself."[10] Vonnegut jumps from how he returned to Dresden in 1967 on a Guggenheim fellowship with his "old war buddy," Bernard V. O'Hare, to what it had been like to try to write about Dresden just after the war, to his first meeting after the war with O'Hare in Philadelphia, to his time teaching in the Writer's Workshop at the University of Iowa. Yet as Reed observes, "There is surprisingly little difficulty in following this seemingly disjointed narrative. The prologue [of] the first chapter, and the quick general guidelines to Billy's life in the second, provide the reader with a strong sense of direction from the outset."[11]

Perhaps most helpful is Vonnegut's discussion in chapter 1 of his failed attempts at writing a traditional narrative about Dresden—one with an Aristotelian beginning, middle, and end:

> As a trafficker in climaxes and thrills and characterization and wonderful dialogue and suspense and confrontations, I had outlined the Dresden story many times. The best outline I ever made, or anyway the prettiest one, was on the back of a roll of wallpaper.
>
> I used my daughter's crayons, a different color for each main character. One end of the wallpaper was the beginning of the story, and the other end was the end, and then there was all that middle part, which was the middle. And the blue line met the red line and then the yellow line, and the yellow line stopped because the character represented by the yellow line was dead. And so on. The destruction of Dresden was represented by a vertical band of orange cross-hatching, and all the lines that were still alive passed through it, came out the other side.

There are many reasons why such a traditional structure did not work for the novel Vonnegut wanted to write, but the principal one is that characters' lives, like those of real people, do not themselves proceed in one direction: in reality one does as much "backward" traveling in time through memory as "forward" traveling in anticipation of the future. Thus while not identical with it, *Slaughterhouse-Five's* narrative mode is allied with the stream-of-consciousness technique pioneered by Joyce and Faulkner, which seeks to reproduce the mind's simultaneous blending of the past through memory, the present through perception, and the future through anticipation. Vonnegut's own life, and Billy Pilgrim's, is characterized by an obsessive return to the past. Like Lot's wife in the Bible, mentioned at the end of chapter 1, Vonnegut could not help looking back, despite the danger of being turned metaphorically into a pillar of salt, into an emblem of the death that comes to those who cannot let go of the past. To get to the heart of the matter of Dresden, moreover, Vonnegut felt he had to let go of the writer's usual bag of chronological tricks— suspense and confrontations and climaxes—and proceed by a different logic toward the future of the novel form.

Thus Vonnegut gives away what would be the traditional climax of his book—the execution of Billy's friend Edgar Derby "for taking a teapot that wasn't his"—in the novel's first paragraph. Throughout the novel he intentionally deflates suspense by mentioning in advance the outcome of any conflict he creates. The readers learn early, for example, that Billy will be kidnapped and taken to the planet Tralfamadore in 1967, where he will learn of the very different ways the Tralfamadorians view the universe. He learns as well that Billy will be shot to death on February 13, 1976, by Paul Lazzaro, a paranoid sadist Billy had been captured with in the war. He even learns with Billy the ultimate fate of the universe: the Tralfamadorians will accidentally blow it up while experimenting with a new type of rocket fuel. Thus, rather than being like a straight line, the narrative chronology of *Slaughterhouse-Five* is more like an ascending, widening spiral that circles over the same territory yet does so from an ever higher and wider perspective. Finally, like most science fiction writers, Vonnegut hopes to push the reader's perceptual horizon as far as he can toward infinity—toward the union of all time and all space. There mystery remains, even though suspense disappears, since suspense is a function of a lack of knowledge at a single point in time and space.

Paradoxically, in creating this cosmic, nonlinear narrative Vonnegut uses fragments of all sorts of traditional narrative forms, much as a bird might use twigs, bits of string, and its own feathers to construct a nest, something very different than the sum of its parts. As Richard Giannone observes, "Graffiti, war memos, anecdotes, jokes, songs—light operatic and liturgical—raw statistics, assorted tableaux, flash before the reader's eye."[12] The most important linear narrative underlying all of these is the Judeo-Christian Bible, which is itself a central motif in *Slaughterhouse-Five.* There time proceeds from the creation to man's fall to the birth, crucifixion, and resurrection of Christ to the end of time with the Second Coming. Giannone suggests that the Gospels were "an amalgamation of language forms that were available to early Christians to spread their good tidings, rather than a fixed ideal shape sent down out of the blue.... [Yet] the old forms were inadequate to convey the momentous news, so primitive Christians made their own."[13] Thus Vonnegut tries in *Slaughterhouse-Five* to do what the Gospel writers attempted to do in their time: construct a new form out of the fragments of old forms.

That Vonnegut was conscious of doing so—that he found the Christian, linear vision of time no longer adequate—is apparent by his remarks in the novel on a book by Kilgore Trout called *The Gospel from Outer Space.* According to Trout, the traditional Gospels are flawed because they seem to suggest that the moral lesson one should learn from Jesus' crucifixion is: *"Before you kill somebody, make absolutely sure he isn't well connected."* In Trout's revised version of the story, rather than being the Son of God, "Jesus really *was* a nobody, and a pain in the neck to a lot of people with better connections than he had. He still got to say all the lovely and puzzling things he said in the other Gospels." Yet when this nobody is crucified, the heavens open up with thunder and lightning, and God announces that he *"will punish horribly anybody who torments a bum who has no connections."* In the course of the novel it becomes clear that the weak, hapless, clownishly dressed Billy Pilgrim is precisely this "bum who has no connections"—that he is in effect a sort of new Christ. Such observations as the fact that Billy lay "self-crucified" on a brace in his German POW boxcar, or that Billy "resembled the Christ of the carol" that Vonnegut takes as the novel's epigraph ("The cattle are lowing, / The baby awakes. / But the little Lord Jesus / No crying he makes.") make clear that this identification of Billy as a Christ-figure is Vonnegut's conscious intention.

Like Christ, Billy brings a new message to the world, although it is a very different one from his predecessor's. And like Jesus he is an innocent who accepts his death, at the hands of an enemy who reviles and misunderstands him, as an opportunity to teach mankind the proper response to mortality. Both Billy and Jesus teach that one should face death calmly, because death is not the end. In the Christian vision the self after death proceeds forward in time eternally, either in heaven or hell; for Billy, however, "after" death the soul proceeds backward in time, back into life. As Billy learns from the Tralfamadorians,

> When a person dies he only *appears* to die. He is still very much alive in the past, so it is very silly for people to cry at this funeral. All moments, past, present, and future, always have existed, always will exist. The Tralfamadorians can look at all the different moments just the way we can look at a stretch of the Rocky Mountains, for instance. They can see how permanent all the moments are, and they can look at any moment that interests them. It is just an illusion we have here on Earth that one moment follows another one, like beads on a string, and that once a moment is gone it is gone forever.

Thus Billy, the new Christ, preaches that human beings *do* have eternal life—even if there is no life after death.

The literary consequence of the Tralfamadorian conception of time is the Tralfamadorian novel, which consists of "brief clumps of symbols read simultaneously." As the Tralfamadorians tell Billy, these symbols, or messages, when seen all at once "produce an image of life that is beautiful and surprising and deep. There is no beginning, no middle, no end, no suspense, no moral, no causes, no effects." *Slaughterhouse-Five* is of course itself an attempt to write this sort of book, as Vonnegut announces in his subtitle: "This is a novel somewhat in the telegraphic schizophrenic manner of tales of the planet Tralfamadore." While human beings cannot read all the passages of the book simultaneously, its short length, its scrambled chronology, its deft juxtapositionings of different times to make thematic points, and its intricate patterns of imagery all combine to give the reader something of that effect. Once he finishes the novel—after a few hours, perhaps in one sitting—the reader can visualize all of Billy's moments stretched out before him like the Rocky Mountains; further, he can see the author's life in the same way, all the way from World War II to the assassination of Robert Kennedy in 1968, when Vonnegut was composing the last pages of *Slaughterhouse-Five*.

Notes

8. Lundquist 71.

9. Stephen F. Hawking, *A Brief History of Time* (New York: Bantam, 1988).

10. Lundquist 75.

11. Peter J. Reed, *Kurt Vonnegut, Jr.* (New York: Warner, 1972) 179.

12. Richard Giannone, *Vonnegut: A Preface to His Novels* (Port Washington, Ny: Kennikat Press, 1977) 84.

13. Giannone 85–86.

KURT VONNEGUT ON DRESDEN (INTERVIEW WITH LEE ROLOFF)

On the afternoon of September 29, 1996, and just hours before the premiere of a stage adaptation of his Slaughterhouse Five, Kurt Vonnegut spoke of his life and work in a far ranging interview and conversation with Lee Roloff, Steppenwolf lecturer for the play discussion series, the PLAY talks.

(...)

Writing Slaughterhouse Five was opportunism, among other things, because after the war, I was trying to make a living as a writer and was looking for "subjects" all the time. I had a family to support. May I say people hate to hear about writing as a business, but it is that. So I am asking myself, "What am I going to do next to make money?" And I thought: Dresden. My gosh, I saw this thing. Heard it. You couldn't see it without being killed. But I could hear it overhead—the firebombing of Dresden. And, also, I thought it was probably a pretty ordinary experience I had been through. I came back from the war to Indianapolis and looked in the February 14th edition of the Indianapolis News about the bombing and all it said was that our planes had been over Dresden that night. And that was all it said! And so I said, "God, that isn't much of a war story!" And then more and more information came out on the scale of this disaster, which I certainly couldn't judge from the ground. And this information came most from the British because in the House of Commons they had debated strategic bombing: was it a good idea or not? It might not be, you know, just on military grounds. To hell with ethics.

And so, ten or more years after I got home, I realized that the Dresden bombing was a pretty fancy event, including the fact that it is a Guinness Book of Records event. Near as anybody knows, it was the largest massacre in human history. I mean Auschwitz was a slow killing process. In order to qualify as a massacre there has to be the killing of a whole lot of people in a very short amount of time. And this was what Dresden was all about: killing about 135,000 people in the course of a night - let's say about eight hours, something like that. So I decided that if I were going to support my family, I should write about it. I was there. I am entitled. And so I started.

I wanted Frank Sinatra and Dean Martin and some of our other war heroes to be in this movie of mine. Duke Wayne, of course. So I tried this and I tried that and it wasn't working and it wasn't working. So I got in touch with some of my war buddies, people who had been there with me. And they wouldn't remember it. They didn't want to talk about it. So I had a particular war buddy who just died about two years ago, by the name of Bernard V. O'Hare. He had become a criminal lawyer. So I went and saw him and on a basis of friendship said to him, "Come on! Let's between us remember as much as we can because I want to write a book!" And his wife suddenly came into the room and was disgusted with the whole enterprise, in fact, was disgusted with the whole human race, and said, "You were just babies then." And indeed we were! And that's where I got the subtitle: "The Children's Crusade." In the anniversary edition of *Slaughterhouse Five* there's an additional subtitle, "A Duty Dance with Death." Well, I had seen a hell of a lot of it. I was teaching at City College in New York recently, and one of my students said she'd never seen a dead person. I said, "Be patient."

Yes, I saw a hell of a lot of death, and I saw a hell of a lot of it during the Battle of the Bulge when my division was wiped out. But then in Dresden I saw a mountain of dead people. And that makes you thoughtful. We were put to work. There were no air raid shelters in Dresden, and we got through it because we were in a slaughterhouse, and in that slaughterhouse there was a huge and very old meat locker dug out of the clay beneath the slaughterhouse. It was probably dug a hundred years ago where they could keep meat cool because they had no refrigeration. But we survived, ironically. And when we came up above ground, everybody else for miles around was dead. Day after day, we were sent into town to take corpses out of cellars because that's where the people went. The Germans did not expect a raid on Dresden. They thought it was an open city, although there is no such city under international law. It was just a dream. Of course, the corpses became a health hazard and we were forced to dig our way down into the cellars because the rubble had closed the staircases. We went down into these cellars and brought out the corpses on stretchers and put them on a big pyre. Believe me, it was a mountain a corpses. And then, when the kerosene was thrown on that pile and touched off - WOOOOOAHHH! It ... made ... you think about ... death. I have said, too, that I would not have missed it for the world. It was a hell of an adventure. You know, as long as you going to see something, see something really thought provoking.

Vonnegut reflects upon Billy Pilgrim, the central character of Slaughterhouse Five.

I based Billy in part upon an experience I had with a very gawky guy with very narrow shoulders who should never have been in the army. His name was Edward Crone. He should never have been a soldier. He didn't look like a soldier, in fact he looked like a filthy flamingo. Yes, he really did look this way. He was a sophomore engineering student at Hobart when he was drafted. He should have been put in limited service, or he should have been classified 4F, or whatever. He wound up, as everybody eventually wound up, in the infantry. All the army needed at that time were riflemen. And ... he died in Dresden. He died of what is called the "thousand mile stare." People did this same thing in prison camps, dying of the thousand mile stare. When one chooses the thousand mile stare, this is what happens: the person sits down on the floor with his back to the wall, will not talk, will not eat, and just stares into the space in front of him. We could not get the Germans to do anything about Edward Crone, and he finally died. And he was buried in Dresden. And the Germans buried him in a white paper suit. Why? Because I guess that is what the burial garments were. After the war, his parents - who were, by the way from Rochester, New York - went over to Germany and returned his body to the United States. He is buried in Rochester now. I paid a visit to his grave about a year ago when I was lecturing in Rochester. And that visit to his grave finally closed out the war for me. I talked to him a little. I know that he gave up to the "thousand mile stare" because life made absolutely no sense to him. And he was right. It wasn't making any sense at all. So he didn't want to pretend he understood it anymore, which is more than the rest of us did. We pretended we understood it.

It seemed important for Vonnegut to explain why the bombing of Dresden was neither a moral nor an immoral act, whereas the killing of a person by another person is a moral act. Could he explain this distinction?

The issue for me is free will. And these opportunities are very rare really. After the bombing of Dresden, and after we came out of our shelter there, we had to walk out of town. It was hot, too, and the stones were hot. Suddenly two American fighter planes peeled off their machine guns as we were moving across the rubble. Now that was immoral I think. It was immoral because the pilots thought we were Germans and it appeared that they didn't have anything else to do and so they thought it would be a kind of fun. I guess they even talked about it on the radio before they peeled off after they saw this thin line of survivors walking across ruins.

The United States, of course, had Chicago. The University of Chicago is famous for performing the first man-made, man-controlled nuclear reaction under the bleachers at Stagg Field. At a memorial service there on the occasion of the fiftieth anniversary of the Bombing of Hiroshima, I came to speak. There was a physicist who had taken part in that tremendous moment in American history, that moment when scientists found out they could make matter behave in this manner. And one physicist who had taken part in the experiment apologized. I found that extremely interesting. Then the question came up as to whether or not we should have bombed Hiroshima. And I said that I had to honor the opinion of my friend, William Starling, who was a Marine in the Pacific. I was in Japan with him when he made his comment, "Thank God for the atom bomb on Hiroshima or I'd be dead now." (You don't want to go anywhere with him overseas because he's liable to say anything.) And I responded by saying that proof that my government can be racist, can behave in a ya-hoo, utterly uncivilized, cruel, nutty manner is ... Nagasaki. Nagasaki had to be just for the fun of it, just for the hell of it because certainly the military point had been made with Hiroshima. For me it was exactly like being strafed by our own pilots in Dresden. And so it goes.

JOSH SIMPSON ON BILLY PILGRIM AND SCIENCE FICTION

> I resent a lot of science fiction. This promising of great
> secrets just beyond our grasp—I don't think they exist.
> —Kurt Vonnegut, interview with Frank McLaughlin, 1973

(...)

Stanley Schatt once remarked that "[j]ust as money is a central character in *God Bless You, Mr. Rosewater*, death serves that role in *Slaughterhouse-Five*," Vonnegut's much-anticipated and long-awaited Dresden book (Schatt 1976, 81). A prisoner of war behind German lines at the end of Word War II, Vonnegut was present when the city was firebombed in February 1945. Although few would deny that *Slaughterhouse-Five* is Vonnegut's undisputed masterpiece, they seem to agree on little else. William Rodney Allen argues that the novel is Vonnegut's "story" of Dresden (Understanding 77–79). William E. Meyer Jr. claims: "[...] [w]e need to concede that *Slaughterhouse-Five* is not, finally, about the fire-bombing of Dresden [...]. Rather, the work stands, albeit stumblingly, in that long line of New-World 'fiery hunts' for self-discovery—for the excitement and horror of 'the great principle of light'" (96). Perhaps the truth lies somewhere between Allen's and Meyer's equally astute observations. I argue that although *Slaughterhouse-Five* on the surface is Vonnegut's Dresden novel, on a much deeper level it is also the story of Billy Pilgrim, a man so tormented and haunted by the burden of the past that he finds it necessary to "reinvent" his own reality. As is the case with Eliot Rosewater, Kilgore Trout's science fiction novels are responsible for Billy's reinvention.

As a result of the unspeakable atrocities and mounds of human wreckage and carnage that he saw in Dresden, Billy, on returning home, checks himself into a "ward for nonviolent mental patients in a veterans' hospital" in the spring of 1948 (127).[1] Pilgrim finds himself sharing a room with Eliot Rosewater, who had voluntarily committed himself to cure his all-consuming drinking habit. In this crucial scene, Vonnegut skillfully links the themes of *God Bless*

You, Mr. Rosewater and *Slaughterhouse-Five*. He states: "[Rosewater and Billy] had both found life meaningless, partly because of what they had seen in war. Rosewater, for instance, had shot a fourteen-year-old fireman, mistaking him for a German soldier. So it goes. And Billy had seen the greatest massacre in European history, which was the fire-bombing of Dresden. So it goes" (128). Vonnegut continues: "So they were both trying to reinvent themselves and their universe. Science fiction was a big help" (128). At this point, readers remember that the action of *God Bless You, Mr. Rosewater* took place in 1965, the year that Eliot Rosewater establishes The Rosewater Foundation. *Slaughterhouse-Five*, however, written four years later than *God Bless You, Mr. Rosewater*, takes readers back in time to 1948 and introduces them to a younger, healthier Eliot Rosewater. Vonnegut's novels build on each other and yield interesting—and sometimes surprising—results when each work is read as a part of a larger whole and not just for itself. In this case, the reader learns that Rosewater's insanity, like Billy's, is brought about by his reinvention of himself and his universe in 1948, three years after the end of World War II.

Kilgore Trout's novels, of which Rosewater has an extensive collection, are the tools with which Billy constructs his new, postwar reality. According to Vonnegut: "Kilgore Trout became Billy's favorite living author, and science fiction became the only sort of tales he could read" (128). This passage echoes Rosewater's comments at the Milford science fiction convention, in which he blurted out to the assembled body of writers, "I love you sons of bitches. You're all I read anymore" (18).[2] Using the novels of Kilgore Trout as their guides, Rosewater and Billy set out on journeys of reinvention. Readers of *God Bless You, Mr. Rosewater* know that Rosewater's journey fills him with dreams of a classless, Marxesque utopia; Billy, on the other hand, journeys to Tralfamadore, a planet in a distant galaxy where free will does not exist.

For years, scholars, critics, and readers of *Slaughterhouse-Five* have been asking whether Tralfamadore exists of whether it is a figment of Billy's warped imagination. One writer suggests, "Billy [...] increasingly withdraws from reality and ultimately loses his sanity" (Broer 88), whereas another argues that "[...] from the moment he comes 'unstuck in time,' Billy continually tries to construct for himself an Edenic experience out of the materials that he garners over the course of some twenty years" (Mustazza 299). Yet another admits that "[t]he novel is so constructed that one cannot determine whether or not what Billy sees is real" (Schatt 65). Vonnegut leaves the question of Tralfamadore's existence open to debate; however, a close reading of the novel strongly suggests that it exists only in Billy's mind, having been placed there by Kilgore Trout's particular brand of literary "poison."

According to Billy, he has been to Tralfamadore many times. He claims that he was first kidnapped by a flying saucer on a clear night in 1967—nineteen years after he first encountered Trout's fiction in the psychiatric ward: "The saucer was from the planet Tralfamadore, [Billy] said. He was taken to Tralfamadore where he was displayed naked in a zoo, he said. He was mated there with a former Earthling movie star named Montana Wildhack" (32). Throughout the novel, it is unclear whether Billy was abducted by a flying saucer or whether he has lost his mind. In 1969, near the end of the novel, a Kilgore Trout novel catches Billy's eye in the window of a New York adult bookshop. He quickly enters the shop and begins inspecting the novel. At this point, Vonnegut breaks into the narration: "He got a few paragraphs into it, and then he realized that he had read it before—years ago, in the veterans' hospital. It was about an Earthling man and an Earthling woman who were kidnapped by extraterrestrials. They were put on display in a zoo on a planet called Zircon-212" (257). Comparing the description of Billy's abduction with the plot of Trout's The Big Board makes it clear that Tralfamadore is nothing more than a product of Billy's mind. He first read the novel in the veterans' hospital in 1948—during the spring of his reinvention. As a result, he created Tralfamadore as a way of escaping his troubled past. In that light, his Tralfamadorian existence must be approached as an escape mechanism grounded in mental instability but—and this is key—fueled by Troutean science fiction.

Slaughterhouse-Five shows two things simultaneously and with equally chilling clarity: what war and bad ideas can do to humanity. War psychologically wounds Billy Pilgrim; however, the ideas contained in Kilgore Trout's science fiction novels are, ultimately, responsible for his complete divorce from reality. Vonnegut, in his next novel, Breakfast of Champions, forces Trout to confront the dangers that exist at the heart of his own printed words.

Notes

1. I intend to use dates whenever possible in order to locate Billy Pilgrim in his own narrative. Because, as the opening line of the novel suggests, he has become "unstuck in time," it is often difficult to tell where he is at any given moment in the novel. Time, not sequence, I argue, is crucial to understanding Pilgrim's progression.

2. It is difficult to keep track of time in Kurt Vonnegut's novels. For example, Vonnegut's comment on Billy (referring to a time in the late 1940s) directly relates to remarks that Rosewater made almost twenty years later (mid- to late 1960s). For the purposes of this essay—and my own sanity—I approach Vonnegut's works in chronological order. Because *Slaughterhouse-Five* was written later than *God Bless You, Mr. Rosewater*, I include in this section any light that the former can shed on the latter.

Works Cited

Allen, William Rodney, ed. Conversations with Kurt Vonnegut. Jackson: UP of Mississippi, 1999.

———. Understanding Kurt Vonnegut. Columbia: U of South Carolina P, 1991.

Broer, Lawrence R. Sanity Plea: Schizophrenia in the Novels of Kurt Vonnegut. Rev. ed. Ann Arbor: UMI Research Press, 1989.

Klinkowitz, Jerome. Kurt Vonnegut. London: Methuen, 1982.

McLaughlin, Frank. "An Interview With Kurt Vonnegut Jr." Allen 66-75.

Meyer, William H. E. Jr. "Kurt Vonnegut: The Man With Nothing to Say" Critique. 29.2 (1988): 95-109.

Mustazza, Leonard. "Vonnegut's Tralfamadore and Milton's Eden." Essays in Literature 13.2 (1986): 299-312.

Schatt, Stanley. Kurt Vonnegut Jr. Boston: Twayne, 1976.

———. "The World of Kurt Vonnegut Jr." Critique 12.3 (1971): 54–69.

Standish, David. "Playboy Interview." Allen 76-110.

Vonnegut, Kurt. *God Bless You, Mr. Rosewater*. 1965. New York: Dell, 1980.

———. "Science Fiction." Wampeters, Foma, & Granfalloons: Opinions. 1974. New York: Delta, 1999.

———. Slaughterhouse-Five. 1969. New York: Delta, 1999.

ALBERTO CACICEDO ON SLAUGHTERHOUSE-FIVE AND CATCH-22

A central issue that World War II raises for novelists is how to represent the ultimately inexpressible horrors of that war and, at the same time, engage the reader in a dialogue that might produce the saeva indignatio (savage indignation) that Jonathan Swift, for example, considered the affective preliminary to ethical social action. Scholars are convinced that Joseph Heller's *Catch-22* leads to such a vision of human responsibility issuing from indignation. As Robert Merrill puts it, "Yossarian deserts because he finally realizes there are greater horrors than physical pain and death" (50). In Heller's own estimate, those greater horrors are "the guilt and responsibility for never intervening in the injustices he [Yossarian] knows exist everywhere" (qtd. in Merrill 51). At the end of the novel, when Yossarian decides to go to Sweden, he does so specifically to run to his responsibilities: "Let the bastards thrive," says Yossarian, "since I can't do a thing to stop them but embarrass them by running away" (Heller 462). In this case, the ethical decision is to estimate what one can credibly do to work against a mad, destructive system and then do it.

Critics of Kurt Vonnegut's *Slaughterhouse-Five*, on the other hand, are not unanimously so willing to grant the ethical engagement of the novel. *Slaughterhouse-Five* has produced two very different schools of thought on Vonnegut's ethical focus. On the one hand, Tony Tanner argues that the novel leads to quietism, which springs from a sense of hopelessness (128). Sharon Seiber appears to associate that hopelessness with predestination and fatalism (148). James Lundquist connects that hopelessness to black humor and argues that such humor is, in effect, an expression of human inadequacy in the face of the complexities of the universe (18–19).1 Such inadequacy, Seiber suggests, can produce only a sort of impotent, uneasy chuckle at Billy's expense but most decidedly not the savage indignation of Swift (152). Robert Merrill and Peter A. Scholl, on the contrary, vehemently oppose the idea that the novel advocates quietism. To be sure, they say, Billy Pilgrim escapes into a quietistic fantasy world (146), but for them, Billy himself is an object of satire. His serenity, they say, is bought at the price of complicity in the "indifference to moral problems which is the ultimate 'cause' of events like Dresden" (148). By contrast, the narrator of the novel, whom Merrill and Scholl take to be Vonnegut, inserts himself into the narrative again and again to demonstrate precisely the distance between Billy's serenity and his own restless, inevitable grappling with the evil of the world. Stanley Schatt differs from Merrill and Scholl to the extent that he makes Billy ultimately as incapable of serenity as Vonnegut himself. Whatever serenity seems to be present in the novel, says Schatt, belongs to a disembodied narrator who sympathizes with the Tralfamadorian view of things, quietistic in the sense that it sanitizes existence by encouraging one to avert the gaze from unpleasant events (87–88). More complex is Tim Woods's argument, derived from Derrida's treatment of history as supplement or "other," that the novel is "a dramatization of Vonnegut's deeply felt need and commitment to justice and ethical responsibility in opening oneself to the other, in recognizing one's indebtedness to the other" (117).2

Leaving aside specific points of disagreement, I concur with those critics who see in Vonnegut, as in Heller, an impulse toward ethical, responsible behavior. However, I argue that the central issue with which the two novels concern themselves is not so much taking responsibility as getting to the point at which responsible action is possible. As I see it, to be ethical requires that one develop Swift's indignation against the injustices of the world and, in the context of these two novels, against the complacencies that lead to depravity and world war. To do that, one must squarely and unblinkingly face the memories of what one must fight against. As an instance of what I mean, consider the decisive moment in Casablanca, when Rick is converted from a self-indulgent cynic to a loving, committed one. At that moment he asks Sam to play—not to play again, but just to play—"As Time Goes By," a song that for Rick opens the doors of memory on a past that had been too painful to remember consciously. As the flashback to that past transpires and Rick, along with the audience, revisits Paris on the verge of German occupation, it becomes increasingly clear that Rick's mutilated emotional life, which we have seen in the first part of the film, is a direct result of the pain of that past. The flashback makes us see that Rick's behavior in Casablanca has been poised delicately between leaving his love behind and still feeling his love as an affliction of the heart. I want to emphasize here that the particular circumstances of Rick's pain are romanticized and, ultimately, too sentimental to carry the burden of what I want to address in this paper. But I begin by referring to Rick's plight because in the refrain of Sam's song, "You must remember this," is the kernel of Freud's double-edged insight into the effects of trauma on its victim. Rick's demand that Sam play the song and his effort finally to contend with a past too traumatic to recollect and yet too formative to leave behind is at the center of what I want to consider in regard to

Catch-22 and Slaughterhouse-Five.

These two novels make the effort to recover memory that is central to their narrative structures. In Catch-22, Yossarian's decision is ultimately, as he puts it, to stop "running away from my responsibilities. I'm running to them. There's nothing negative about running away to save my life" (461, emphasis in original). But that decision comes in the final chapter of the novel, specifically at a point in the narrative when Yossarian has finally remembered, clearly and with no ambiguities, the death of Snowden, the central traumatic event of his career as bombardier. Heller, in fact once said, "Snowden truly dies throughout Catch-22" (qtd. in Merrill, 46). That comment points to the fact that, throughout the entire novel, Yossarian's memory has worked its way around Snowden's death, giving the reader flashes of the event, sometimes as off-handed references but more often as grotesquely comical ones like the sudden eruption of the phrase, "Where are the Snowdens of yesteryear" (Heller 35–36). But until the full revelation of the event in the next-to last chapter, Snowden's death is never actually recollected or enacted in its full horror. To the extent that they puzzle the reader and make Yossarian seem bizarre beyond understanding, one result of those sometimes comical prefigurements of the horror is that they serve as "a kind of trap," as Merrill puts it, that makes the reader complicit in the carelessness of the General Dreedles and Colonel Cathcarts of this world. Then, when the horror becomes clear, the recurrence of the references to the event effects a conversion in which "we come to feel something like shame for our indifference" (Merrill 47, 53). Thus, the indignation that we felt at the horrors produced by self-interested officers turns inward and prompts in us a desire to act against those horrors. It is, however, important to recognize that throughout the novel Yossarian is as much in the dark as is the reader about the actuality of Snowden's death. The novel circles around and around the death precisely because Yossarian can neither remember it nor forget it.

In that sense, Snowden's death is for Yossarian like Ilsa's abandonment for Rick—although the implications of Snowden's death are much more serious. David Seed has analyzed the lesson of Snowden's death, as finally recollected by Yossarian. At that moment, as Seed reminds us, Yossarian quotes Edgar's remark in King Lear, "the ripeness is all." But Seed points out that the circumstance of Snowden's death "blocks off" the sense that the passage has in Lear, the attempt to induce a philosophical acceptance of death. On the contrary,

> One important metaphysical theme of Catch-22 is the physical vulnerability of man. [...] Death in this novel is presented as a conversion process whereby human beings become mere matter and are assimilated into the non-human. [...] Snowden [...] spills his guts, which happen to be full of ripe tomatoes, and so Heller implies that man may become no more than the fruit, vegetables and meat he consumes. Where Edgar pleads for acquiescence, however, Heller sets up Yossarian as a voice of refusal, of resistance to the inevitability of death. (Seed 41)

As Merrill concludes, Snowden's secret is that "[i]t is the spirit that counts, not 'matter'" (52)—and Yossarian's acceptance of the responsibility to stay alive is, in effect, a paradoxical affirmation of the spirit's capacity to transcend the limits of matter. Thus, Yossarian's remembering becomes the impetus for the ethical challenge that he takes up in the final chapter. In that regard, it is worth noticing that in a book in which, for the most part, the names of characters are the titles of chapters, not until Yossarian remembers Snowden's death is a chapter titled "Yossarian"—the final chapter in some sense, because Yossarian finally acts rather than reacts.

One could argue that the first chapter of *Slaughterhouse-Five* begins where the final chapter of Catch-22 ends. The subject of that first chapter is precisely the real, biographical difficulty that Vonnegut encounters in attempting to remember the bombing of Dresden, the central traumatic event of his novel. The chapter is really pure autobiography. In a 1973 interview with David Standish, Vonnegut acknowledged that for some time he was unable to remember the actual bombing of Dresden: "[T]here was a complete forgetting of what it was like[...] the center had been pulled fight out of the story" (70). Not until that failure of memory is made good can Vonnegut write *Slaughterhouse-Five*—and, Merrill and Scholl argue, precisely because Vonnegut can write such a book, he takes an ethically responsible stance that denies the quietism of Tralfamadorian philosophy. In a literal contradiction of the Tralfamadorian ethos, he pointedly looks at those "unpleasant" moments, not because he revels in them but because they so powerfully determine who he is and what he does. Vonnegut's admiration for Lot's wife, who does look back (21–22), underscores the point. The first chapter of *Slaughterhouse-Five* makes clear that, as with Rick's and Yossarian's, Vonnegut's memory of trauma had not disappeared. On the contrary, if the absent presence of trauma produces Rick's cynicism and Yossarian's madness—for I think one has to agree with Seed that until the moment of remembering, Yossarian is indeed mad (33)—then the repressed memory of the bombing of

Dresden produces in Vonnegut a "disease," as he calls it in the novel:

> I have this disease late at night sometimes, involving alcohol and the telephone. I get drunk, and I drive my wife away with a breath like mustard gas and roses. And then, speaking gravely and elegantly into the telephone, I ask the telephone operators to connect me with this friend or that one, from whom I have not heard in years. (4)

The symptoms of Vonnegut's disease reproduce the dynamic of trauma: the alcohol deadens the memory that the phone calls seek to arouse. If one takes Merrill and Scholl's position that Vonnegut, as he inserts himself into the novel, is a man with "greater resources" than weak, quietistic Billy Pilgrim in *Slaughterhouse-Five* (146)—in effect, that Vonnegut is like Yossarian at the end of Catch-22—then one must also acknowledge that Vonnegut's recovery of the memories that will enable ethical action is a mighty struggle against the impulse to suppress and repress.

Addressing the symptomatology of trauma in his book, *Beyond the Pleasure Principle*, Freud describes the case of a little boy who, traumatized by being abandoned by his mother, reenacted the scene of the trauma over and over and over again. So striking was the event for Freud that it forced him to reconsider his original, relatively unproblematic idea of the pleasure principle, which had indicated that people who experienced traumatic events would avoid them or any object that might recollect the trauma (9). Working through the implications of the little boy's reenactments, Freud concluded that, for a child, such repetitions may reflect a self-conscious effort to dominate the traumatic event, for, he said, children "can master a powerful impression far more thoroughly by being active than by merely experiencing it passively" (29). But when the repetition is not a conscious reenactment of the traumatic event, the fact of repetition points toward neurosis (30). And, said Freud, the more powerful the trauma-precipitating event, the more likely that the conscious memory will be repressed as too dangerous for the psychic well-being of the individual, and the more likely that those repressed memories will express themselves in unconscious reenactments of the traumatic event (14–15).

Yossarian's behavior before recollecting Snowden's death and Vonnegut's behavior in trying to remember the bombing of Dresden duplicate the symptomatology of trauma that Freud described. The fictional character and the real novelist must revisit the traumatic event over and over again precisely because it has determined their lives in profound ways; yet, because of its horrific power, the event has also erased itself from their consciousness. The narrative structure of Catch-22, like that of Vonnegut's own life, is determined by vertiginous circlings around their respective central traumatic events. As James Mellard says of Yossarian, "[I]t is the protagonist's moral life, his inner-life, his psychological needs that account for the novel's delaying tactics" (36, emphasis in original). Once having achieved a clear memory, the result for the traumatized person is therapeutic in the sense that it enables him to confront the horror that he has endured and to act on that knowledge. So too, about his own experience Vonnegut says that writing the novel "was a therapeutic thing. I'm a different person now. I got rid of a lot of crap" (qtd. in McGinnis 56). Freud said that the task of the therapist who is treating trauma is "to force as much as possible into the channel of memory and to allow as little as possible to emerge as repetition" (13). I am not confusing the therapy that Freud and Vonnegut mean with the "don't worry, be happy" school of latter-day psychobabble. The Tralfamadorians speak from the position of psychobabble therapy: Don't dwell on bad moments; don't worry, be happy. On the contrary, as Merrill and Scholl make clear, the therapeutic aspect of Vonnegut's experience in remembering Dresden is to arouse the indignation that makes it possible to write *Slaughterhouse-Five*, a self-consciously, relentlessly anti-war book, written at the height of the Vietnam War, and geared to argue specifically against that war as well as against war generally (147 and passim).

In his book on the Holocaust, Dominick LaCapra considers the motivation to tell and retell the story of so horrible an event and concludes that "one may entertain the possibility of modes of historicity in which trauma and the need to act out (or compulsively repeat) may never be fully transcended but in which they may to some viable extent be worked through and different relations or modes of articulation enabled" (14n10). To paraphrase LaCapra's terminology, retelling the story need not be neurosis and is positively therapeutic if it works toward making the teller or the reader conscious of the past and therefore able to work against the cause of the trauma—in the case of LaCapra's book, the Holocaust; in the case of Heller and Vonnegut, the horrors of World War II generally. From that point of view, the writing of *Slaughterhouse-Five* is like Yossarian's taking off for Sweden, not a running away from responsibility but an acceptance of responsibility according to the capability and limitations of the individual concerned.

Works Cited

Althusser, Louis. "Ideology and Ideological State Apparatuses (Notes Towards an Investigation)." Lenin and Philosophy and Other Essays. Trans. Ben Brewster. New York: Monthly Review P, 1971. 127-86.

Boon, Kevin A. "The Problem with Pilgrim in Kurt Vonnegut's *Slaughterhouse-Five*." Notes on Contemporary Literature 26.2 (1996): 8-10.

Casablanca. Dir. Michael Curtiz. Perf. Humphrey Bogart, Ingrid Bergman. Paul Henreid, and Claude Rains. Warner Brothers, 1942.

Freese, Peter. "Vonnegut's Invented Religions as Sense-Making Systems." The Vonnegut Chronicles: Interviews and Essays. Ed. Peter J. Reed and Marc Leeds. Westport, CT: Greenwood, 1996. 145-64.

Freud, Sigmund. Beyond the Pleasure Principle. Trans. James Strachey. Standard Ed. New York: Norton, 1975.

Heller, Joseph. Catch-22. New York: Dell, 1985.

LaCapra, Dominick. Representing the Holocaust: History. Theory, Trauma. Ithaca, NY: Cornell UP, 1994.

Lundquist, James. Kurt Vonnegut. Modern Literature Monographs. New York: Ungar, 1977.

McGinnis, Wayne D. "'The Arbitrary Cycle of *Slaughterhouse-Five*: A Relation of Form to Theme." Critique: Studies in Modern Fiction 17.1 (1975): 55-68.

Mellard, James M. "Catch-22: Deja vu and the Labyrinth of Memory." Bucknell Review 16.2 (1968): 29-44.

Merrill, Robert. Joseph Heller. Twayne's United States Authors Series. Boston: Twayne, 1987.

Merrill, Robert, and Peter A. Scholl. "Vonnegut's *Slaughterhouse-Five*: The Requirements of Chaos." Critical Essays on Kurt Vonnegut. Ed. Robert Merrill. Boston: Hall. 1990. 142-51.

Schatt, Stanley. Kurt Vonnegut, Jr. Twayne's United States Authors Series. Boston: Twayne, 1976.

Seed, David. The Fiction of Joseph Heller: Against the Grain. New York: St. Martin's, 1989.

Seiber, Sharon. "Unstuck in Time: Simultaneity as a Foundation for Vonnegut's Chrono-Synclastic Infundibula and Other Nonlinear Time Structures." Kurt Vonnegut: Images and Representations. Ed. Marc Leeds and Peter J. Reed. Westport, CT: Greenwood, 2000. 147-53.

Standish, David. "Playboy Interview: Kurt Vonnegut, Jr.," Playboy July 1973: 57-60+.

Tanner, Tony. "The Uncertain Messenger: A Reading of *Slaughterhouse-Five*." Critical Essays on Kurt Vonnegut. Ed. Robert Merrill. Boston: Hall. 1990. 125-30.

Vonnegut, Kurt. *Slaughterhouse-Five* or the Children's Crusade: A Duty-Dance with Death. New York: Dell, 1971.

Woods, Tim. "Spectres of History: Ethics and Postmodern Fictions of Temporality." Critical Ethics: Texts, Theory and Responsibility. Ed. Dominic Rainsford and Tim Woods. New York: St. Martin's, 1999. 105-21.

Notes

1. Thus, also Seiber, who suggests that "Billy has been stripped of his humanism through the devastation of war" (149).

2. Woods argues persuasively that later Derrida presents the same case, that simultaneously feeling the present of an alienated past is essential to "justice" and "responsibility." See especially Woods's quotation from Derrida's Specters of Marx: "No justice—let us not say no law and once again we are not speaking here of laws—seems possible or thinkable without the principle of some responsibility, beyond all living present, within that which disjoins the living present, before the ghosts of those who are not yet born or who are already dead. [...] Without this non-contemporaneity with itself of the living present [...] what sense would there be to ask the question "where?" "where tomorrow?" "whither?'" (qtd. in Woods 119; emphasis in original).

Works by Kurt Vonnegut

Player Piano, 1952; published as *Utopia 14* (1954). Published again as *Player Piano*, 1966.

The Sirens of Titan, 1959.

Canary in a Cathouse (stories), 1961.

Mother Night, 1961.

Cat's Cradle, 1963.

God Bless You, Mr. Rosewater; or, Pearls before Swine, 1965.

Welcome to the Monkey House: A Collection of Short Works (stories), 1968.

Slaughterhouse Five, 1969.

"Penelope." 1960. Later revised as "Happy Birthday, Wanda June," 1970.

Breakfast of Champions; or, Goodbye Blue Monday, 1973.

Wampeters, Foma, and Granfalloons: (Opinions) (essays), 1974.

Slapstick; or, Lonesome No More, 1976.

Jailbird, 1979.

Palm Sunday: An Autobiographical Collage (essays), 1981.

Deadeye Dick. 1982.

Nothing Is Lost Save Honor: Two Essays, 1984.

Galápagos: A Novel. 1985.

Bluebeard, 1987.

Hocus Pocus, 1990.

Fates Worse than Death: An Autobiographical Collage of the 1980s, 1991.

Timequake, 1997.

Bagombo Snuff Box: Uncollected Short Fiction (stories), 1999.

Like Shaking Hands with God: A Conversation about Writing, 1999

God Bless You, Dr. Kevorkian, 1999.

A Man Without a Country, 2005

Annotated Bibliography

Broer, Lawrence R. *Schizophrenia in the Novels of Kurt Vonnegut.* Tuscaloosa: The University of Alabama Press, 1989.

Broer offers a psychoanalytic study of Vonnegut's novels beginning with *Player Piano* and going through *Bluebeard*, emphasizing the importance of Vonnegut's actual experience for the construction of his fictions.

Goldsmith, David H. *Kurt Vonnegut: Fantasist of Fire and Ice.* Bowling Green, OH: Bowling Green University Popular Press, 1972.

In this survey of Vonnegut's work up through *Slaughterhouse-Five*, Goldsmith argues that in Vonnegut's novels pilgrims beset by obstacles search for purpose and messiahs in a world that both offers and frustrates meaningfulness.

Hipkiss, Robert A. *The American Absurd: Pynchon, Vonnegut and Barth.* Port Washington, N.Y.: National University Publications Associated Faculty Press, 1984.

Hipkiss examines the problems of purpose and morality in Vonnegut's novels in the context of other writers like Albert Camus and Samuel Beckett who postulate an absurd and amoral world.

Klinkowitz, Jerome. *Vonnegut in Fact: The Public Spokesmanship of Personal Fiction.* Columbia, SC: University of South Carolina Press, 1998.

Presents a study of Vonnegut's work in the context of his utterances as a public figure concerned with social, political, civic, and spiritual issues.

Leeds, Marc. *The Vonnegut Encyclopedia: An Authorized Compendium.* Greenwood Press, 1994.

This is a comprehensive descriptive catalogue of characters, themes, images, and phrases found in Vonnegut's work.

Matheson, T. J. "This Lousy Little Book: The Genesis and Development of *Slaughterhouse-Five* as Revealed in Chapter One," *Studies in the Novel* 16 (1984): 228–240.

Argues that the themes and structural characteristics of *Slaughterhouse-Five* are previewed in the first chapter and thus help to orient readers to the peculiarities of the rest of the novel.

Mayo, Clark. "*Slaughterhouse Five* or Wonderful New Lies." In *Kurt Vonnegut: The Gospel from Outer Space, or Yes We Have No Nirvanas*. The Borgo Press, San Bernardino, CA, 1977.

Considers Vonnegut's use of an outer space alien's perspective to examine social and religious values and practices.

Morse, Donald E. *The Novels of Kurt Vonnegut: Imagining Being An American*. Praeger, 2003.

Morse discusses how Vonnegut's novels reflect the major traumatic public and private events that have gone into imagining being an American during the twentieth century. He focuses how Vonnegut deals with the Great Depression, World War II, nuclear weapons, the Vietnam War, changing social institutions, marriage, the family, divorce, growing old, experiencing loss, and anticipating death.

Mustazza, Leonard. *Forever Pursuing Genesis: The Myth of Eden in The Novels of Kurt Vonnegut*. Lewisburg, PA: Bucknell University Press; London and Toronto: Associated University Presses, 1990.

In a survey study of the pursuit of paradise in Vonnegut's novels, Mustazza discusses Tralfamadore as a version of the Garden of Eden and Billy and Montana Wildhack as versions of Adam and Eve.

Reed, Peter J. and Marc Leeds. The Vonnegut Chronicles: Interviews and Essays. Greenwood Press, 1996.

Contains a chronology of Vonnegut's life, interviews with him, and critical essays about his work, his craftsmanship, and his ideas. The volume also includes examples of Vonnegut's graphic art.

Contributors

Harold Bloom is Sterling Professor of the Humanities at Yale University. He is the author of 30 books, including *Shelley's Mythmaking* (1959), *The Visionary Company* (1961), *Blake's Apocalypse* (1963), *Yeats* (1970), *A Map of Misreading* (1975), *Kabbalah and Criticism* (1975), *Agon: Toward a Theory of Revisionism* (1982), *The American Religion* (1992), *The Western Canon* (1994), and *Omens of Millennium: The Gnosis of Angels, Dreams, and Resurrection* (1996). *The Anxiety of Influence* (1973) sets forth Professor Bloom's provocative theory of the literary relationships between the great writers and their predecessors. His most recent books include *Shakespeare: The Invention of the Human* (1998), a 1998 National Book Award finalist, *How to Read and Why* (2000), *Genius: A Mosaic of One Hundred Exemplary Creative Minds* (2002), *Hamlet: Poem Unlimited* (2003), *Where Shall Wisdom Be Found?* (2004), and *Jesus and Yahweh: The Names Divine* (2005). In 1999, Professor Bloom received the prestigious American Academy of Arts and Letters Gold Medal for Criticism. He has also received the International Prize of Catalonia, the Alfonso Reyes Prize of Mexico, and the Hans Christian Andersen Bicentennial Prize of Denmark.

Neil Heims is a freelance writer, editor and researcher. He has a Ph.D in English from the City University of New York. He has written on numerous authors including John Milton, Arthur Miller, William Shakespeare, Albert Camus, and J.R.R. Tolkien.

Peter J. Reed is a well-known Vonnegut scholar and a Professor in the Department of English at the University of Minnesota.

Stanley Schatt has taught in the English Department at the University of Houston and has written on Herman Melville and Native American literature.

Richard Giannone is a professor of English at Fordham University and the author of several book-length studies of Flannery O'Connor.

James Lundquist has written about Sinclair Lewis and Edgar Allen Poe as well as Vonnegut.

William Rodney Allen holds a Ph.D from Duke University, teaches at the Louisiana School for Math, Science, and the Arts, and besides Vonnegut has written about Walker Percy and Flannery O'Connor.

Lee Roloff is Professor Emeritus of Performance Studies at Northwestern University. He taught performance art, archetypal and psychological approaches to literature, and literature in the therapeutic setting. He is a published poet and writer and created and inaugurated the PLAYtalks series at the Steppenwolf Theatre in Chicago.

Josh Simpson teaches in the English Department at Eastern Kentucky University.

Alberto Cacicedo is Professor of English at Albright College and has written extensively on Shakespeare.

Acknowledgments

"The End of the Road: *Slaughterhouse-Five or The Children's Crusade*" by Peter J. Reed. From *Kurt Vonnegut, Jr.*, by Peter J. Reed, pp. 178–180; 187–192. © 1972 by Warner Books. Reprinted by permission.

"Vonnegut's Dresden Novel: *Slaughterhouse-Five*" by Stanley Schatt. From *Kurt Vonnegut, Jr.*, by Stanley Schatt, pp. 88–89; 94–96. © 1976, Twayne Publishers. Reprinted by permission of The Gale Group.

"*Slaughterhouse-Five*" by Richard Giannone. From *Vonnegut: A Preface to His Novels* by Richard Giannone, pp. 86–93. Copyright © 1999 by Richard Giannone. Used by permission of the author.

"The 'New Reality' of *Slaughterhouse-Five*" by James Lundquist. From *Kurt Vonnegut* by James Lundquist, pp. 71–78. © 1977 by Continuum International Publishing Group, Inc. Reprinted by permission

William Rodney Allen, "Slaughterhouse-Five," In *Understanding Kurt Vonnegu*t, Columbia: University of South Carolina Press, 1991, pp. 81-89. Reprinted by permission of University of South Carolina Press.

Lee Roloff, "Kurt Vonnegut on stage at the Steppenwolf Theater, Chicago." (Interview) *TriQuarterly*, Fall 1998, i.103, pp. 17-18. Reprinted by permission of the author.

Josh Simpson, "This Promising of Great Secrets": Literature, Ideas and the (Re)invention of Reality in Kurt Vonnegut's *God Bless You, Mr. Rosewater*, *Slaughterhouse-Five*, and

Index